The Art of the Good

On the Regeneration of Fallen Justice

VALENTIN TOMBERG

The Art
of the Good

On the Regeneration
of
Fallen Justice

✠

Translated by
Stephen Churchyard
James R. Wetmore

✠ Angelico Press

First published in German as
Degeneration und Regeneration der Rechtswissenschaft
© Verlag Götz Schwippert, Bonn, 1946
Reprinted by Bouvier Verlag, Bonn, 1974
First published by Angelico Press, 2021
English translation by Stephen Churchyard
and James Wetmore © Angelico Press, 2021
Introduction © James Wetmore, 2021

For information, address:
Angelico Press
169 Monitor St.
Brooklyn, NY 11222
angelicopress.com

ISBN 978-1-62138-687-2 (pbk)
ISBN 978-1-62138-688-9 (cloth)
ISBN 978-1-62138-689-6 (ebook)

Cover Design: Michael Schrauzer

CONTENTS

Introduction

Part I
The Degeneration of Jurisprudence & Its Causes

Part II
The Nature of True Jurisprudence

Part III
Towards the Regeneration of Jurisprudence

Introduction

*Overview of Valentin Tomberg's Life**

VALENTIN TOMBERG was born in St. Petersburg on February 26, 1900.[1] Having been baptized a Protestant, he entered the Greek Orthodox church shortly before 1933, and, in 1945, became a Roman Catholic. His father, Karl Arnold Tomberg, was the administrator of a high school in St. Petersburg, and worked from 1903 onwards as an official in the Russian ministry of the interior.

After attending St. Peter's School, where he was given a classical education, with teaching conducted in both Russian and German, Tomberg studied one semester at the Faculty of Law at the University of St. Petersburg, but the Russian Revolution of November 1917 prevented his further studies. During his life, Tomberg learned to speak fluent Russian, German, French, English, Dutch, and Estonian, and had a good command of Spanish, Polish, Ukrainian, Latin, Greek, and Church Slavonic. In 1918 he fled with his family to Estonia. There his mother, Juliana Umblia, was shot and killed by the Bolsheviks, an event that left deep marks on Tomberg, and shaped his view of communist Russia for the rest of his life. In 1920 he moved to Tallinn, where, between 1928 and 1938, he worked as an interpreter in the postal service administration.

---

* We gratefully acknowledge our debt to Michael Frensch for his permission to incorporate in this Introduction material he first published in *Valentin Tomberg, Band I.2. 1944–1973* (Novalis Verlag, 2005).

[1] According to the Julian calendar then used in Russia the date was February 14th, that is, St. Valentine's day.

A lifelong friendship bound him to the Russian poet Nikolai Belozvetov (1892–1950). In 1925 Tomberg joined the Estonian Anthroposophical Society, becoming its vice-president in 1926, and its president in 1932. From the beginning of the 1930s he began to publish essays in anthroposophical journals. In 1933, he married Maria Belozvetova (1893–1973) in Tallinn, and in the same year his son Alexis (1933–1995) was born. Towards the end of that year there appeared the first of his twelve "anthroposophical meditations on the Old Testament"; twelve further such meditations on the New Testament followed between 1935 and 1937. Both sets of essays divided opinion in the Anthroposophical Society, since in them Tomberg developed his own spiritual inquiries, which in part went beyond Steiner.[2]

In 1938 Tomberg emigrated to the Netherlands and began actively to lecture on Christological topics.[3] Until the Russian occupation of the Baltic states in 1940 he earned his living as a secretary in the Estonian Vice-Consulate in Amsterdam; thereafter, he was dependent on the support of friends. In the middle of July 1940 he began to teach a weekly course on the Lord's Prayer to this circle of friends.[4] This course, which was organized as a series of meditative exercises affording deep insights into the secrets of Christian esotericism, was broken off in 1943 because of the threat posed by German occupying forces.

---

[2] Valentin Tomberg, *Christ and Sophia, Anthroposophic Meditations on the Old Testament, New Testament & Apocalypse* (Great Barrington, 2006).

[3] Two of these lecture series were later published in book form: *Sieben Vorträge über die innere Entwicklung des Menschen,* and *Die vier Christusopfer und das Erscheinen des Christus im Ätherischen* (the former was published in English as *Inner Development,* most recently in 1992; the latter, under the title *The Fours Sacrifices of Christ,* is contained in the volume mentioned in note 2).

[4] Published by Achamoth Verlag in 4 volumes as *Der Vaterunser-Kurs* and subsequently in English as *The Course on the Lord's Prayer.* An earlier translation by Robert Powell is available at sophiafoundation.org. A new translation is in preparation by Angelico Press for publication in 2021.

The longer the war went on, the more Tomberg sought to find an organization or community with a Christian basis that had not been to some extent corrupted or destroyed by National Socialism; he found it at last in the Catholic Church. Tomberg's trust in this institution rested, first, on its established hierarchy and its seven sacraments; and, second, on the fact that there was a whole series of Catholic men and women who had offered resistance to the Nazis, and who had paid the price by perishing in concentration camps.

At the beginning of 1944 Tomberg moved to Cologne at the invitation of the legal scholar Ernst von Hippel (1895–1984), whose friend he had become, and in the same year he was awarded the title of Doctor of Law for his dissertation on "The Degeneration and Regeneration of Jurisprudence,"[5] here published in English for the first time in a readily accessible edition. A work on international law followed at the beginning of 1945.[6] These two books were published in 1946 and 1947 respectively, in editions of 15,000 and 5,000. In February 1945 Tomberg began work on his *Habilitationsschrift*, because he was clearly working towards an academic career. This new work on international law was intended to be his contribution to the new German constitution. It was completed in November 1948, by which time, however, Tomberg was already living in England, and so was unable to defend it according to the required academic protocols. Neither could he find a publisher for the work, and, in 1950, he destroyed it, since he saw it as no longer relevant.

[5] Published in 1946 by Verlag Götz Schwippert, Bonn. Reprinted in 1974 by Bouvier Verlag, Bonn.

[6] *Die Grundlagen des Völkerrechts als Menschheitsrecht*. Published in 1947 by Verlag Götz Schwippert, Bonn. A translation into English as *The Foundations of International Law as the Law of Humanity* is in progress by Angelico Press.

The law professor Fritz von Hippel (brother of Tomberg's close friend Ernst) suggested to Tomberg in 1949 that he should write another work on international law.[7] This text was finished only at the end of 1952, and is to appear for the first time in 2021 in the original German under the title *Vom Völkerrecht zur Weltfriedensordnung*.[8] Thus, Tomberg's four works in the field of jurisprudence were the fruit of a period of activity lasting from 1944 to 1952. More will be said regarding these works, and the events of Tomberg's life during which they were written, later in this introduction.

In July 1945, Tomberg, with his wife and son, moved into a camp for "displaced persons" in Ossendorf, Cologne. There he worked for the British Army as a translator. In 1946 he became a lecturer at the technical college in Aachen, specializing in ethics and law. From the summer of 1947 onwards the Tomberg family lived with the Belozvetov family in Mülheim, in the Ruhr. There Tomberg led the reconstruction of the state high school. In 1948 he moved with his family to London, and, a year later, to Reading, where he worked until 1960 as a translator for the BBC, and continued to write on international law, as well as on religious and intellectual-historical topics. In 1952 he became a British citizen.

Between the years 1958 and 1967, Tomberg composed in French the text he is best known for, *Méditations sur les 22 arcanes*

---

[7] *Die Problemgeschichte der Völkerrechtswissenschaft*, typed manuscript.

[8] The Herder publishing company had planned an omnibus of articles by various authors on the topic of the history of international law, and Fritz von Hippel asked Tomberg whether he would like to contribute to it, but it appears he misconstrued the inquiry to mean he was being asked to compose a separate work on the subject. Only after completing this task did he learn that Herder had made no such request, and would not undertake its publication. Once the first German edition of this text is published in 2021, Angelico Press will commence an English translation of it, under the title *From International Law to World Peace*.

majeurs du Tarot,[9] now considered a spiritual classic of the twentieth century, and for which Hans Urs von Balthasar wrote an Afterword and Robert Spaemann a Foreword. Tomberg's final works, written in German, were published posthumously.[10] He died on February 24, 1973, on the island of Majorca, and was buried in the cemetery in Palma de Mallorca.

Tomberg's Works on
Jurisprudence & International Law

As stated in the overview of Valentin Tomberg's life, more remains to be said regarding his life and work in the context of this first in a series of his works on true *justice* to be published by Angelico Press—works composed during, and in the aftermath of, the holocaust of World War II. At that time, in which all social and legal order was in a worsening state of collapse, Tomberg nonetheless single-mindedly pursued his legal studies at the University of Cologne, working determinedly towards his doctorate. At first sight, it seems hardly credible that such a topic could be chosen and permitted at a university in a totalitarian state—in which, day in and day out, the greatest *injustice* was taking place, and in which Nazi control over the academy had long been a *fait accompli*. But the University of Cologne was an exception, and by July 1944 Tomberg was already being entrusted with the tasks of an academic assistant in the Institute for International Law by the trustees of that university.

---

[9] In English, *Meditations on the Tarot: A Journey into Christian Hermeticism,* republished in an expanded edition by Angelico Press in 2020.

[10] Published in 1985 by Verlag Herder Basel as *Lazarus komm heraus! Drei Schriften von Valentin Tomberg.* A revised English translation of this work, entitled *Lazarus Come Forth!,* is scheduled for publication by Angelico Press.

Although work could not then take place at the university itself, because of what was happening in the war, he continued to study at home, close to Bonn and Bad Godesberg.

During this time, Tomberg finalized the topic of his dissertation as "The Degeneration and Regeneration of Jurisprudence," and the composition of this text was to take place under even more unbelievably exacting conditions. Although Bonn and Bad Godesberg had not previously figured as prime targets in the battle plans of the British and American air forces, all this changed utterly in October 1944. The Western allies wanted to test a new and improved version of their radio bombing system, for which three conditions were needed: a previously undamaged city center, a location on a river, and bad weather at the time of the attack. The first and second conditions made Bonn an ideal target. And when the third condition was met, on October 18, 1944, the old town of Bonn was destroyed. Incredibly, it was immediately after this raid that Tomberg applied to be permitted to take the oral examination for his doctorate before completing his dissertation. In addition to this, he had enlisted in the emergency services and had been called into action on the Siegfried Line, where he had contracted pyelitis and cholecystitis.

This dissertation, his first writing on jurisprudence, marks an important turning-point in Tomberg's life. Humanistic studies which he had presented during his thirties in anthroposophical terminology are now replaced by a strict orientation towards a Platonic model of knowledge, and a medieval, so-called "realism of universals."[11] With the assistance of Goethe's phenomenological method, Tomberg tries to show that the spiritual or intellectual substance of law is a reality, making reference to Rudolf Steiner's approach to epistemology in the

[11] *Universalien-Realismus.*

latter's early work, *Die Philosophie der Freiheit*.[12] He describes law as an organism having several different levels, corresponding to the different levels of conceptuality: the *ideal* of law, the *idea* of law, and the actual *concept* of law, over which the two other levels take precedence. A correct appreciation of positive law, obligatory for the administration of justice, has to rest on a concept of law that is itself derived from the idea of law, which, in turn, originates in the ideal of law.

Philosophical analyses, and analyses in the history of law, led Tomberg to regard the modern path away from a natural law founded upon religion, and towards a legal positivism oriented towards power, as a dismantling of the different levels of law and, at the same time, as a loss of both the *idea* and the *ideal* of law. This dismantling amounts to a process of *degeneration*. In Tomberg's dissertation, which reveals him as a Christian humanist thinker, he also proposes a new way of organizing the academic study of law, in which the higher levels of law would be included, and in which access to the idea and the ideal of law would be restored.

* * *

The subject of his dissertation, however, points to yet another turning-point in Tomberg's life. Whereas he had mainly concentrated, throughout his time in the Netherlands, on anthroposophical and humanistic studies and ways of thinking, where what was at the center of his interests and activity was what happened within the Anthroposophical Society and the anthroposophical movement, his attention now turned to the situation of humanity as a whole, and thereby to that of each and

---

[12] Various editions of this work have appeared in English, under the titles *The Philosophy of Spiritual Activity* (Steiner's preferred translation of his title), *The Philosophy of Freedom*, and, more recently, *Intuitive Thinking as a Spiritual Path*. ED.

every individual human being, regardless of their particular affiliations. Thus did Tomberg extend his field of inquiry and interest to humanity as a whole and its destiny, which brought with it a turn in his orientation towards the Universal Church with its hundreds of millions of members, a Church concerned with the affairs of all humanity. Alongside the Eastern Orthodox Church, Tomberg took the Roman Catholic Church to be the most important representative of the Universal Church. Indeed, in his dissertation he gave prominence to the Roman Catholic Church, with its monarchical, aristocratic, and democratic elements, as an example of a true community.

Indeed, it may even be said that it was precisely this widening of his field of inquiry that led Tomberg to questions of law and to a scholarly engagement with them. For in Tomberg's eyes, the human catastrophe of the Second World War was a consequence of the overthrow of law by overbearing states conscious of their own power, above all by Bolshevist Russia and Nazi Germany. This overthrow of law, opportunistically tolerated by the mass of legal scholars and lawyers, if not directly justified by them, was not, for Tomberg, something essentially inexplicable that had come out of the blue, but was rather the directly necessary consequence, precisely, of the *degeneration* of jurisprudence and of the practical law founded upon it—a degeneration that had begun in the medieval controversy between realism and nominalism, had continued in the Renaissance and Early Modern period, had led to the European revolutions, and had culminated in the modern totalitarian state. And as we have seen, Tomberg was at this stage encountering this degeneration day in and day out in a Cologne more and more devastated by each successive Allied attack. He wished to work against this onslaught in his jurisprudential studies, in order to contribute to a *regeneration* of jurisprudence, and, thereby, to a regeneration of law as well.

* * *

In a central passage of his dissertation, Tomberg cites Leibniz's view regarding the connection between the level of law or justice and the levels of human community. At the first level, men live and strive for the realization of true happiness through individual perfection; at the second level they strive for shared perfection as a community; at the third level, they live, as a community, in communion with God. What should be noticed here is that Leibniz's final goal is not that the church should be absorbed into the state, but that the state should become a church. A "state church" would, therefore, be the complete opposite of Leibniz's conception. What hovers before him as the future goal that is to be striven for is not the gradual absorption of the church into the state, but the gradual absorption of the state, with its economic and political special interests, into the church, which would be no other than the realization of the Augustinian *City of God*.

This unification of different elements which the present text so strongly foregrounds as being, in Leibniz, a feature of the nature of substance and knowledge themselves—a unification that makes it possible peacefully to reconcile what are at first sight mutually contradictory worldviews—will, along with a model of knowledge and of spiritual behavior divided into different levels, become in Tomberg's late work, *Meditations on the Tarot: A Journey into Christian Hermeticism*, a fundamental feature of the nature of substance and knowledge themselves. Leibniz is referred to in that text also, supplemented there by an Hermetic exposition of the divine name *Yod-He-Vav-He*, in which each of the four divine letters is assigned its own level of knowledge with a particular sense-organ. The "jurisprudential phase" of Tomberg's life can therefore also be seen as containing the seeds of this late work.

★ ★ ★

Tomberg's second jurisprudential work, *The Foundations of International Law as the Law of Humanity*, was essentially conceived, and, in part, also written, at the turn of the year in 1944–45, which is to say during a time in which, as with his dissertation, the uninterrupted droning of four-engined bombers, and exploding bombs that often shook the doors and windows, provided a continual reminder of the immediate proximity of death, prompting that seriousness of disposition which only the proximity of death and of great suffering can bring with it. Emerging from that solemn moment, this second work is particularly intended for readers who have, even today, retained this serious mood, that is to say, for readers who are conscious of their responsibility for the happiness and unhappiness of the community of mankind, and who understand that the idol of unlimited arbitrary power must be overthrown, and in its place must be brought into force an international law that is no longer state law—that is, a product of the state's arbitrary power—but is an enforceable law of humanity that stands above the states. Thus, the "law of humanity" *breaks* or overrides the law of states: and the intention of this second book was to make its own decisive contribution to the establishment, dissemination, and realization of this truth of experience. It was dedicated to all the innocent victims of unlimited state sovereignty across the whole world—and, in particular, to the fresh graves of children in Warsaw, Rotterdam, Belgrade, London, Coventry, Kiev, Odessa, Sevastopol, Cologne, Hamburg, Stuttgart, and dozens of other cities where children lay buried as victims of "total war" from the air—as did the mothers of these children.

As in his dissertation, Tomberg in this text also seeks to develop his topic from deep-laid knowledge of a worldview. In his doctoral thesis he had set out the degeneration of jurisprudence against the background of the four essential elements of law prescribed by Thomas Aquinas: that is, the eternal law set above everything else, the *lex aeterna*, which lives as divine law (*lex divina*) in the divine and spiritual world, and which sets out the true *ideal* of law, is mirrored in the natural law (*lex naturalis*) as the *idea* of law which is innate to human reason, and which, when related to the experience of the reality of human life in practice, is given expression in the *concept* of law, or the law which is positively in force (*lex humana*).

In light of the above, which recalls Tomberg's repeated appeal to tradition as an indispensable element both in any regeneration of true justice, and in countering evil, we note that already on February 2, 1943, in the context of his course on the Lord's Prayer, Tomberg had suggested to his friend Mariä Lichtmess in Amsterdam the "building of an ark":

> In the present day we are experiencing the rise of over-powering evil, a kind of Flood. The awakening of evil is an inundation: it is directly at work in everyday consciousness. In such a Flood it is a case of sink or swim. This is the trial that consciousness is undergoing. Rescue, however, comes from the principle of the ark.
>
> What is it to build an ark? It is to build in consciousness a four-square edifice, whose length, breadth, and height are such that they can contain everything in the whole expanse of life. All cultural values and truths are to be gathered and conserved in extract. Unextinguished recollection of everything essential in the good and true. This is the life-raft that will prevent us from drowning. Now, when the darkness has come up over humanity's head, it is a question of carrying the ark in one's consciousness, that is, of remembering all the essential values of culture. The result of this is that man will not wither in the life of his soul, his life-body: he will remain alive with his soul. From the carrying of the ark of recollection within come faith, hope, and

love. When a truth has become so strong that it enters into our spiritual body, it becomes faith, hope, and love.[13]

With these words is sketched one of Tomberg's key concerns in the second half of his life: the thread of tradition is not to be broken, but rather all that is true and precious in the history of mankind is to be collected and grasped in its wisdom and depth. Only on this basis is it possible to plant strong new impulses in history. The recent past, precisely, had sufficiently shown that any will to renewal would end in catastrophe if it did not honor the context out of which it was working and within which it was situated. And for Tomberg it was beyond doubt that the context in which European history stood and within which it could be understood was Christianity. Only out of Christianity, out of the structures that had originated in it, and out of its fundamental virtues, could real renewal be hoped for.

★ ★ ★

Before completing our survey of this "jurisprudential" season in Valentin Tomberg's life and work, let us revisit his conversion to Catholicism near the outset of this period. An essential reason for Tomberg's conversion, as has been briefly mentioned before, was the fact that in the time of Nazi dictatorship the Catholic Church was the only institution he trusted to create a spiritual counterweight to all the abominations this dictatorship had set in motion. He could thus identify with the values of the Catholic Church. We have only a few pieces of evidence of his faith from the war years, mostly from Hippel's letters, but in these we read a number of times that he attended Holy Mass with Tomberg whenever possible. That the work which both Hippel and Tomberg were undertaking was at a

---

[13] Final entry of the *Lord's Prayer Course*, 1943.

high religious and philosophical level can also be gathered from the letters. In Tomberg's case, these ideas clearly influenced his jurisprudential writings. Thus, in the present book we read:

> What distinguishes the Catholic Church is that it serves the goal of the conservation and nurture of tradition in a very intensive way, yet at the same time it participates no less intensively to shape and contest all areas of contemporary life—and that it strives towards an ideal of the future that embraces all mankind. Out of all known larger human communities, the Catholic Church is the most perfect in this respect: it never forgets the past, but works and takes care for the future, and adopts an active position towards all the events of the present day. . . . How is the fact of the superiority of the Catholic Church to all other human communities in this respect to be explained? In my view the reason lies in the fact that it is the Catholic Church that most corresponds to the requirements for a harmonious state of society. . . . It is the most democratic community, since every son of a peasant can in principle achieve the highest station, the papacy; it is at the same time the most aristocratic community, since it is constructed in a strictly hierarchical fashion; it is arranged more plurally than any other community—one need only think of the many lay and monastic orders with their varied rules and regulations—yet at the same time it displays a unity among all the different races and nations of the world, a unity that could never be attained or preserved by force, but could only be brought about, and will only be brought about, by virtue of a unity of values (of religious belief, for example).

* * *

As we have seen, in his second book, *The Foundations of International Law as the Law of Humanity*, which he sometimes described as *International Law I*, Tomberg had already written about the inevitability that the law of humanity, or international law, would break or override state law whenever the latter legitimated injustice and inhumanity. After this followed what he would refer to as *International Law II*, which he undertook at an unpropitious moment—Germany before the passing of the Basic Law—and the manuscript of which he later burnt. In this work, Tomberg had hoped to make an effective contribution to the provision of a constitution to a new Germany emerging from the ruins of National Socialism, and, indirectly, to help provide such a constitution to Europe also.

In his fourth book on law, *Die Problemgeschichte der Völkerrechtswissenschaft*,[14] Tomberg then brought together the *history* of international law in a more general, strongly philosophical overview—that is, he formulated his results in such a way that they are not only fruitful for the special case of the existing constitutional arrangements of a particular state, but in principle serve in general the peaceful life together of *all* states on earth governed by true reason, actual justice, and lived humanity. If Tomberg, in his first text on law showed how an *ideal* of law, an *idea* of law, and a *concept* of law together constituted the *essence* of law, in this, his fourth, he shows (as was noted earlier) that each of these was considered alike and in its due place by Thomas Aquinas, in the form of *lex aeterna* or *divina*, *lex naturalis*, and *lex humana*—that is, *eternal* or *divine* law, *natural* law, and *positive* law. And if in his first text he demonstrated the loss of the *ideal* and the *idea* of law in the law currently in force in the modern age, in this latter work Tomberg describes the gradual dismantling of Aquinas's edifice of law as an "eclipse"

---

[14] See page 4, including notes 7 and 8.

of *divine* and *natural* law in modern international law—a process that began as a purely methodological exercise, but led in due course to the *actual* eclipse of the higher vocation of international law, until it was understood purely positivistically as a legitimation of power, and even, on occasion, served towards the misuse of international law by the absolutely sovereign modern state.

Let us further summarize. With his four studies on jurisprudence (or, perhaps better said, on true justice) with specific reference to international law, Tomberg built a sort of four-storey edifice with a particular ordering. If his *Degeneration and Regeneration of Jurisprudence* was his tersely expounded sketch of and path towards *contact* with the integral *essence* of law as an *ideal type*—in that it exhibits vertically a three- or even four-storey building which had, in the course of the history of law in the West, been dismantled and forgotten, and which therefore had to be remembered again and to be reintegrated into a true understanding of law; if his second book, *The Foundations of International Law as the Law of Humanity,* was the *realization* of the higher levels of a binding law of humanity, so that its result could be formulated as follows: the law of humanity *breaks* or overrides the law of the state; if his third book (the so-called *International Law II*) was designed to have an *effect* in a particular historical situation, the effect of regenerating the substance of a German law that had declined and finally been destroyed in the Nazi period; then the fourth, *From International Law to World Peace,*[15] his most philosophical book, can be thought of as a bringing-together or *summa* of Tomberg's jurisprudential research and insights.

---

[15] As mentioned before, to be published in 2021 for the first time in German as *Vom Völkerrecht zur Weltfriedensordnung*, and in due course in English as *From International Law to World Peace.*

What can be seen for the first time in these four books, books written, in part, amid the most dramatic war-time circumstances, is the four-step ladder—*contact, realization, effect, philosophical summa*—which Tomberg was later to expound in detail in the first four Letters of his most important work, *Meditations on the Tarot*, under the concepts of *mysticism* (contact), *gnosis* (realization), *magic* (efficacious action), and *hermetic philosophy* ("teaching"), and whose significance for an integral human knowing he was to present with deep and comprehensive clarity to a new generation.

JAMES WETMORE
MICHAEL FRENSCH
St. Valentine's Day, 2021

Preface

THE PRESENT STUDY was written in Autumn 1944—that is, at a time when tyranny and war prevailed. Although times have changed, I have not found it necessary to alter either the study's content or its wording. The events of the year and a half since then have in many ways provided fresh corroboration of the work's theses; in no respect, however, have these theses been weakened, let alone refuted.

The study originated from a suggestion of Prof. Ernst von Hippel. Numerous conversations with him (some of them in the emergency shelter of the house in which we were both living at the time) regarding the topics discussed here provided a further valuable contribution to the work's development. I am therefore delighted to have the opportunity to express my deeply felt gratitude to Prof. von Hippel here.

PART I

The Degeneration of
Jurisprudence & Its Causes

Quantitative & Qualitative Thinking in *Natural Science*; Mechanical & Moral Thinking in *Jurisprudence*

T HE QUARREL that Goethe began with Newton and his disciples in the field of color theory is significant not only for physicists or for Goethe scholars, but for all thinking human beings—and therefore for lawyers as well. For it displays with perfect clarity a case in which two different people make use of different organs to investigate the *same* object. Whereas Newton considered any appearance as "explained" or "known" when the phenomenon appearing in it (color, for example) could be replaced by a formula consisting of *calculable quantities*, Goethe on the other hand regarded a given appearance as "known" when whatever was remote from human beings in the phenomenon could be connected to a phenomenal element standing in close proximity to them, and which could be humanly experienced.

The task Goethe sets himself in the course of knowing something consists in his starting from a phenomenon observed in the external world and then moving it *towards human beings* through a series of connecting phenomena, until, ideally, it culminates as something that appears in a purely interior, moral, and conceptually transparent way to our inner life. At this point the process of cognition has reached its goal: that which stands outside, which is alien, and for this reason dark and enigmatic, has become something interior, known, and therefore explained.

What Newton seeks is the opposite of this. He is "centrifugal" with respect to the inner man. Newton expects the process of knowledge to achieve such a distance from human beings themselves that the latter, ideally, become equal to zero. Such an exclusion of the human can only be attained however if all *evaluating* activity on the part of the knower is suppressed, that is, if we renounce the *qualitative* aspect of the appearance and grasp it in a manner that is *devoid* of qualities. But this is possible only if something can be found to substitute for quality. Such a substitute is *quantity,* which can be expressed in numbers. For Newton, and therefore for all of academic physics for nearly two and a half centuries, color and light thus become numbers expressing the fluctuations of a something that is hidden behind them. This something, however, is devoid of qualities. It is indeed so devoid of qualities that it does not even need to be given a number in order to figure in the formula. For the purposes of the formula, all that is needed are its fluctuations. And it is of no consequence whether this something is called "ether" or anything else: the quantitative formula fits so many appearances, in order to "explain" them—that is, in order to transform them into quantities—that the "fluctuating something" can in practice be disregarded.

For Goethe however this "fluctuating something" is what knowing the colors of light is all about. For it is not *hidden behind* the colors, but *reveals* itself through them. Colors express the substance of light; they herald its essence. "Colors are deeds done by and to light," says Goethe—and, with this, he declares that for him it is a question of the one who is doing and done to, that is, of just that which quantitatively-oriented cognition relegates to the domain of inconsequential insubstantiality.

"It is instructive that so many men with such profound and acute minds," marvels Goethe, "could not see how a calculation can be in complete accord with the phenomena, whilst yet, for just that reason, the theory that explains the phenomena can be false. In practice, we experience this every day; yet in science, at the summit of philosophy upon which we stand, and upon which, albeit with a little wobbling, we are grounded, such mistakes should no longer occur" (Goethe, *Naturwissenschaftliche Schriften*, ed. R. Steiner, vol. 4, 24). Goethe appeals to the tribunal of the future, which will appear "perhaps in twenty years time," and "before which this question will be aired and will be justly examined and decided" (237). Now, however, nearly two hundred and twenty years have elapsed, and the "tribunal of the future" is still marveling that Goethe, a "man of profound and acute mind," could have created and defended such a scientifically untenable theory of color—just in the way that Goethe himself marveled over the Newtonians and their "impure, hypothetical, false doctrine," and, indeed, was able to clear "their rubble" away.

This conflict of Goethe with Newtonianism past and present is instructive, in that we can, as it were, sound out in it the fact of two essentially different kinds of knowledge. Newton's thinking was oriented towards *quantity*. For him, to know is to convert the qualitative aspects of a phenomenon into a quantity. Goethe's thinking starts out from *quality*. For him, to know is to transform the externally qualitative aspects of a phenomenon into an inner quality, that is, in the final analysis, to elevate them to the status of *moral* values. Such "elevation" does not however consist in *inserting* a human value-judgement into the object, but, on the contrary, in the object's making an ever stronger and clearer impression on human beings by being brought closer to them. That is, such an impression, made first on our eye and our other senses, but which then also impresses itself ever more deeply upon our feelings until at last it reaches the essential core of our human nature, creates a *moral impression*. Such a deepening of the impressions received from the objects we experience is however the opposite of what is taken for "superficiality." A perception or an experience is superficial, rather, when we content ourselves with a fleeting and incomplete impression on the senses, and then arrive at an equally incompletely substantiated judgement about the object. The deepening of perception—passing through all the layers of the human being until it reaches our essential moral core—is however a long road and presupposes such a great measure of interest, attentiveness, and patience that its claim to be *serious, fundamental*, and *scrupulous* must be granted. What for example would the verdict of a judge in a criminal court be worth, if it were based *only* on the obvious, bare facts of the matter, instead of attending to whether these facts result from deliberate design or from negligence on the part of the accused, or to whether he is sound of mind—in other words, whether the fact of the crime signifies the *guilt* of the perpetrator? And what meaning would "equitable appraisal" have, other than the rule of arbitrary whim, if there were no moral judgement that possessed objective validity and rested on a perception internalized to the point of attaining moral significance? What meaning would "equitable appraisal" then have in discerning "mitigating circumstances" in a given case, or in determining whether one is dealing with "murder" or "manslaughter," or in any legal matter where *bona fides* (good faith) has to be known, required, and protected? For even if we leave to one side the question whether Goethe or Newton was right about physics, we *cannot* leave to one side the question whether, in the field of *law*, the thinking which shall apply is to be *quantitative* or *qualitative*. In every nation that has arrived at law's highest state of clarity—that is, *jurisprudence*—this question has been answered in a resolutely definite way by the representatives of justice. *Jus est ars boni et aequi*: law is the art of the good and the just (Cel-

sus, in libro primo *Instit.* Ulpiani). *Jurisprudence*, however, ele-
vates this art to a conscious discipline—that is, to a methodical
and progressive construction of a temple of justice continued
over generations, a temple in which that which transcends
humanity, the divine, allies itself with humanity for the latter's
well-being, for the well-being of states, nations, families, and of
every individual human being.

*Juris prudentia est divinarum atque humanarum rerum notitia,
justi atque injusti scientia*: Jurisprudence is the knowledge of
divine and human things, the science of justice and also of
injustice.

This is the answer which the juridical consciousness of Justinian's Rome gives to the question whether *moral* or *mechanical*
thinking is to be applied in the field of law. This consciousness
was the mature fruit of a growth spanning nearly a thousand
years, and bore within itself the results of the work of hundreds
and thousands of reflective and experienced lawyers. It is neither youthful high spirits nor enthusiastic idealism that speaks
in the *Corpus Juris Justiniani*, but the ripening of a thousand-
year-long experience gathered in the time of the theocratic
priest-kings as well as in that of the aristocratic and democratic
republics, and that of the Caesars' imperial tyranny, pagan and
Christian, and that had been tested and examined by Romans,
Hellenes, and barbarians in Europe, Asia, and Africa. And *this*
experience chose as the formula with which to epitomize its
essence: *Juris prudentia est divinarum atque humanarum rerum
notitia, justi atque injusti scientia*.

The Historical "Fall" of Jurisprudence From the Heights of Religiously Grounded Natural Law Into the Depths of a Positivism Grounded in Power

WHEN COMPARED WITH the resolute Justinian formula, grounded in experience, the formulas that deviate from it, arrived at under the influence of eighteenth-century Enlightenment philosophy and of the nineteenth century's natural-scientific approach to thought, seem ephemeral. For apart from the scholastic doctrine of natural law (which was and still is essentially only an internalization and deepening of the Justinian conception of law) and, additionally, the natural law of religious rationalism represented by Hugo Grotius, Samuel Pufendorff, Christian Thomasius, G.W.F. Leibniz, and Christian Wolff (which still moves within the framework of the tradition), the domain of the great temples has been abandoned and we have arrived at a region of houses and shacks, and, latterly, of barracks and dungeons.

If we contemplate, for example, the grandly comprehensive edifice built by Thomas Aquinas—in which *lex aeterna*, the divine *essence* of law in God, stands on high, and *lex divina*, positive divine law (the next level below *lex aeterna*) represents the *revelation* of eternal law to humanity, so that it may in turn arrive at the level of *lex naturalis*, that is, the level of human *reason*, on the basis of which the decrees of *lex humana*, of positive law, are formulated by the legislator called to that vocation—then we have to admit that here *all* the levels of law are embraced in a single whole.[1] Even as early as the work of Pufendorff (1632–1694) this building is no longer a temple, but a synagogue, a religious "school," since he does away with the highest level, the *lex aeterna*.[2] But when we come to the French representatives of Enlightenment philosophy and to Friedrich Justus Thibaut (1772–1840), who can be seen as the leader of the natural law school in Germany, the building of law loses another storey: the revealed divine law, *lex divina*. All that remains is a purely human, two-storey habitation in which human reason hands down guidelines from the upper storey to the workshop of positive law that is found on the lower floor. But this third layer of legal consciousness, too, was brought to an end by modern *positivism*—which however had already been heralded by Thomas Hobbes (1588–1679), and which had been prepared for by the nominalist current of medieval thought, as also by the sophists of the Socratic era.

In sum, three of the levels of the earlier range of legal consciousness had by now been eliminated, and humanity was delivered up defenceless to the remaining area of "legislation" by the various tendencies of political power. For if *law* no longer traces its binding validity back to absolute divine law and to the dictates of universal human reason, it can *only* rest on force. Thus the development of modern legal consciousness begins with the temple of scholasticism (which was not yet nearly finished, but to which much building work could and should have been added) and ends with dungeons and barracks,

---

[1] Cf. *Summa theologica* 1a2ae, qq. 91 ff.
[2] *Apologia*, §19.

the *force majeure* of the interested parties—that is, with unscru-
pulous positivism in its final and true shape.

In order to understand this path more deeply in its essence,
it is first of all necessary to take a closer look at the main currents of thought in the philosophy of law. These main currents,
in the nineteenth century and the first quarter of the twentieth,
are, besides the continuation of the scholastic current and the
rationalistic school of natural law, the historical school, socio-
economic materialism, and pure positivism.

The historical school sought in something irrational (that is,
in the effects produced by national spirit in history) the basis on
which a philosophy of law free from the conceptions of natural
law could be built up, and nurtured. It renounced the pure
sources of reason, out of which the secularized natural law
movement had created the ideas of law; and in the subconscious influence of the dark impulses shaping the destinies of
nations it saw the workings of the intelligence that created culture and law. This school was especially dominant in the world
of German legal thought up until the middle of the nineteenth
century, after which it had to yield its place to the materialist
current of legal thought.[3] That it had to do so was really a logical necessity proceeding from the *direction* that was taken by
the jurisprudence of the nineteenth (and indeed as early as the
second half of the eighteenth) century. For if rationalistic natural law—in which religion, ethics, and law were one, and in
which reason was taken to be the light of lights, to be divine—
separated out human reason by *emancipating* it alone as the
source of legal ideas, it was natural then that a justified suspi-
cion of this presumptuous elevation of human reason should
come about, and that, in order not to return to the old religious natural law and its culture of reason, it should seek in the

---

[3] R. Stammler, *Lehrbuch der Rechtsphilosophie* (1922), §16.

irrational liberation from a discredited *rationalism*. Thus did the historical school came into being.[4]

Since, however, this school ascribed the shaping of the life of legal ideas to unconscious forces, it paved the way with an inner necessity for the rise of *materialism*. For if the guiding and shaping element was to be found in a domain *outside* consciousness, why should not the basic instincts of matter, which had meanwhile been discovered by biology, just as well be made the foundation as the no less opaque and extra-conscious forces of, for example, "national spirit"? Once the step from consciousness into the extra-conscious had been made, it was impossible to stand midway between them: one had then either to take the path back to religious natural law (whether early-modern, medieval, or ancient Roman),[5] or proceed further into the domain, first of the extra-conscious, then of the subconscious, and finally of the unconscious—that is, of "mat-

---

[4] It came into existence in the year 1815 with the publication of an introductory essay by Friedrich Karl Savigny (1779–1860) in the *Zeitschrift für geschichtliche Rechtswissenschaft*.

[5] The religious natural law, for example, of a Cicero: "This, then, as it appears to me, has been the decision of the wisest philosophers—that law was neither a thing contrived by the genius of man, nor established by any decree of the people, but a certain universal principle, which governs the entire universe, wisely commanding what is right and prohibiting what is wrong. Therefore they called that aboriginal and supreme law the mind of God . . . on which account it is that this law, which the gods have bestowed on the human race, is so justly applauded. . . . For even then, he [Tarquin] had the light of reason deduced from the nature of things, that incites to good actions and dissuades from evil ones; and which does not begin for the first time to be a law when it is drawn up in writing, but from the first moment that it exists. And this existence of moral obligation is co-eternal with that of the divine mind. Therefore the true and supreme law, whose commands and prohibitions are equally authoritative, is the right reason of the sovereign Jupiter" (Cicero, "On the Laws," in *The Treatises of M.T. Cicero*, trans. C.D. Yonge [London: Bohn, 1853], 431–32).

ter." In this way a domain of legal thinking that had turned its back on a reason experienced as *cosmic* light had necessarily to devolve into biological materialism (Haeckelianism) and then also into historical materialism (Marx, Engels).

Thus originated the *socio-economic* current in jurisprudence, which however is only a form of materialism. It is impossible to place the instinctive above reason for any length of time without arriving at its substratum, the "instinct of instincts," that is, "matter." Equally, it is impossible to place the rational over the instinctive for any length of time without arriving at the "sun of the light of consciousness," that is, God as the primal ground of everything rational and moral. One or the other direction has to be taken: that is, either the direction from the rational to an ever-intensifying rationality, until one falls silent in awe before absolute reason (God)—or the direction from the rational to the instinctual, the path of ever-diminishing reason, until one arrives at what is absolutely devoid of reason, at what is absolutely automatic (matter). Whatever may be said or ventured, it will be impossible to avoid the decision whether one wishes to orient oneself towards absolute reason (God) or towards absolute unreason (matter).

Jurisprudence, therefore, was also unable to avoid facing this decision. And for the most part it chose to travel from the light of reason towards the darkness of instinct. This choice however had its own inevitable consequences. If thinking is torn from its natural connection with the moral and the religious, and oriented instead towards the so-called "mere facts" and the "primal instincts" of "experienced reality," it relinquishes all gravity and inner value and becomes a mere tool used for purposes one selects or one considers to be demanded by the facts or by other people. Thinking that is areligious and amoral becomes purely formal and technical. The apparatus of thinking becomes thereby a compliant tool for the instructions one gives it or which are given it from outside. The *depth* of thoughts disappears. Thoughts become mere schematic handles with which one orders things in this way or that. If in this way thinking becomes a shadow, then the *will* is necessarily foregrounded as something more significant and decisive than thinking. But the will is no shadow such as thought has become. Indeed, it drives and moves the apparatus of thinking also, determining thought's direction towards its goal. This psychological experience—that a thinking which has become technical is shadow-like and ineffective—then overshadows the rest of the human being with this inner experience of its own ailing conscious life. Just as thought in this case is only an expression of the *will*, which both incorporates facts and is then in turn influenced (stimulated, constrained) by facts, so the ideas of law, of legal systems and laws, are nothing other than *formulas of will*.

Here, then, there is no such thing as *law* itself, but only whatever suits the will of whoever is in power at any given moment. *Positivism* is, therefore, in its most consistent form, a voluntarism. It is the fruit of that tree whose root is the "autonomy of human reason" (rationalism), whose trunk is the orientation of this autonomous reason towards the instinctive, whose branches are the discovery of this instinctive element in a matter devoid of reason, and whose fruit, finally, is the supremacy of arbitrary rule, the glorification of force. Positivism, to which this developmental direction necessarily leads, is however the end of law, and with it, of jurisprudence, in the world. For *law* is the power of the moral idea of *justice* in the world, a power that tames, masters, and overcomes force and arbitrary rule, a power that humanity inherited from its heavenly Father as the essential feature of His image and likeness, which humanity bears within itself.

The Fall of Jurisprudence Considered in Connection With the Three Temptations in the Wilderness

If law, ethics, and religion are considered as an articulated *unity*, it is impossible to avoid seeing a kind of Fall in the history of nineteenth- and twentieth-century jurisprudence. It is a Fall indeed, which gradually succumbs to the same *three temptations* to which Christ was subjected in the wilderness.[6] For to deviate from the ideal of reason and take the direction towards the instinctual is, *morally* understood, nothing other than to leap from the pinnacle of the temple in the hope that, *there*, an angel of the Lord (an intelligence at work in the darkness of instinct) will *bear up* the one who falls, so that he not "dash his foot against a stone." The summit of pure thought (the "pinnacle"), which is oriented towards the divine (the "temple"), is really abandoned, in order to find in the instinctive (in the "depths") the power of "national spirit" (the "angel"). This however is the path from faith to superstition. For faith, as the imprint of the absolutely good upon human thinking, *also* possesses the sunclear certainty of reason. If, finally, everything creative is rooted in love (in the last analysis hatred can only destroy), then the creation of the world is God's act of love. This love embraces *all* his creatures, who, without it, would not be there at all. This love does not cease with their coming into being, but accompanies them throughout their path of life and death. This care for the welfare of *all* creatures is the *divine* law (the *lex aeterna* of the scholastics). We obey this law because we have the most perfect inner certainty that it realizes, protects, and calls for the welfare of *all* humanity. It is to *this* law that we orient ourselves in all questions concerning human or humanitarian welfare. And although it takes great effort and much work

[6] Matt. 4, 5–7; Luke 4, 9–13.

to fashion a line connecting the summits of religious truths to the legal and practical singularities of life, this work and effort are well worth it because they signify the application of the certain good to life, and indeed the application of the certain good *for everyone* to life.

Faith, therefore, means the sacredness of reason, and certainty in works. Here we know what we are holding to, and *why* we are holding to it. And we know too that what is good for the individual can be deduced from what is good for everyone.

The case is otherwise with, for example, *historicism*. If we place our trust in the sway of a national spirit that is at work through generations, unconsciously determining them, how can we then be sure this national spirit will direct these developments towards the welfare of *all*, that there will not one day arise a conflict between what is produced by the national spirit and the rest of humanity—a conflict arising precisely as a result of the national spirit's efforts? How can we be sure the national spirit is not a *demon* leading people through the centuries towards disaster? For if the *personal* instincts of individuals can be bad, why cannot *national* instincts be bad too?

However the matter may stand, it is always a *risk*, a leap into the unknown, when we entrust ourselves to the guidance of an instinctive force that is at work in a people, since this force is *opaque* and *not* universally valid, but limited. To take such a risk is however the inner essence of superstition, as opposed to faith, and it is superstition that is at work in the world in a thousand ways as the *temptation* to leap from the pinnacle of the temple into the depths, so as to be borne up by the angels.

The historical school fell victim to this temptation when it placed the irrational above reason—the consequences of which followed necessarily as a matter of logic. The leap into the irrational was taken in the hope of being borne up there by angels. But there was no intervention on the part of the "angel." And so the leap took place unobstructed, and ended, as do all leaps, upon the *ground*, that is, with the cult of matter, with *materialism*.

It is not a case of the *same people* who belonged to the historical school becoming materialists (for this was not the case) but only that the *current* of jurisprudence, as it developed further, became materialist. One generation shapes the destiny of the next. And the destiny which the "historical generation" shaped was the "materialist generation" of the middle and the second half of the nineteenth century. The approach of this generation of philosophers of law and lawyers was such that the material and the mechanical fundamentally determined their "superstructure," that is, the cultural and the moral. And it developed, accordingly, a practice that had the aim of setting the lower higher and the higher lower. The *revolutionary* movements of the nineteenth century were all rooted in the conception that the material is primary, and culture secondary. They set the mechanical above the moral, the quantitative above the qualitative.

When seen from a moral point of view, this is however nothing other than the essence[7] of the temptation in the wilderness to turn *stones into bread*. For the transformation of the inorganic, dead stone into organic bread is by its essence an *inversion* of the higher and the lower. To attribute to the stone the property of nourishing won from the grain would be to do in the area of *nourishment* what is done in that of *culture* when the spiritual (law, ethics, religion) is considered and treated as a *product* of the material (of the amoral, and that which is devoid of reason). This however is how materialism in both its branches, the biological and the economic, treats the relation of spirit and matter: it seeks to turn stones into bread.

---

[7] Matt. 4, 3–4; Luke 4, 3–4.

The materialist generation, too, shaped its destiny in the form of the next generation. This generation is still alive today [1944] and can be described as the "positivistic generation." For law is, in the eyes of this generation, what is volitionally *posited* through an authoritative decision and sanctioned by force. And for it, what holds "good" is whatever leads to the goal it has posited. The goal it has posited is, however, its "truth." This generation is no longer materialist, but has, rather, gone a step *further*. For even in the natural-scientific theoretical material-ism of the nineteenth century, the idea of static, uniform, col-orless matter had changed into that of *force* (or the potential for force): bodies consist of molecules, the molecules are produced by vibrating atoms, atoms are the result of electrical vibrations, and electrons are nothing other than pure energy, force as such. Man, too, belongs in this world. In *man*, however, there is a potential for force, a potential that lies at the basis of the whole essence of humanity. This is the *will*. The will is conse-quently the *reality* of human life. In the last analysis it creates and determines *everything*, the whole life of culture and the life of law included. For the life of law, however, this signifies a drastic change in its whole basis. Instead of *law*, we have *power*. Now, this change in meaning signifies no other than the temp-tation in the wilderness, in which the tempter led Jesus Christ to a high mountain, and, showing him "all the kingdoms of the world, and all the glory thereof," promised him *power* over all this if he would fall down and worship him. Now, falling down before, and worshipping, the *principle of power* is just what posi-tivism does—or, in its milder form, is what it leads to.

Symptoms of the Degeneration of Jurisprudence and Its Effects on Jurists and Laymen

T HE FACT OF THE "Fall" of jurisprudence, that is, of the change in its underlying tone and standard, did not go unnoticed by public opinion. In many lay circles the view spread that jurisprudence produced a less valuable kind of human being, who was, from one point of view, cold and hard, and who was, from another, sophistical—bending, morally, "whichever way the wind blew." And indeed the modern lawyer is intransigently committed to formalities ("cold" and "hard") when considering morally significant matters. But he is pliable, compliant, and ready to compromise when faced with matters that have yet to be formally specified, but whose moral content permits only a "yes" or a "no." The lawyer is represented, in other words, as a person for whom what is humanly essential is a matter of indifference, and for whom the inessential is the main thing.

Such a conception is further strengthened and disseminated by judgements such as that a will is to be considered null and void because the testator, say, wrote it on a sheet of paper with the letterhead "Hotel Fürstenhof, Berlin W., Potsdamer Platz,"[1] or because he added "Berlin, 26 February 1916," when

---

[1] *Kammergericht* of April 6, 1916, *Oberlandesgericht* 34, 303. See Fritz von Hippel, "Formalismus und Rechtsdogmatik" (1935), 20.

in order to be correct he should have written "Berlin, West End."[2] Such wills were declared null and void "for lack of a personal signature" (*Bürgerliches Gesetzbuch*, §2231) even though there was not the slightest doubt about who the testator was or about the content of his last will, or indeed even about the place where the will was drawn up.

But however shocking such decisions may appear to the layman, to many lawyers they seem neither harmful nor pointless, but instead justified and purposive, since, to quote Gustav Radbruch, "even the unjust law is not pointless . . . even irrespective of its justice, law already serves an end by being in force, the end of certainty about what the law says. Whoever wants to reconcile himself with jurisprudence must take hold of the law in this spirit."[3] It is therefore, in terms of "legal policy," more important *that* a judgement be arrived at, *that* a case should be decided in agreement with the applicable law in force (even if that law should be inadequate in the particular case), than that the case should be settled *justly*, insofar as the provisions of the law with respect to the need to serve justice have been subjected to a supplementation, or rather an alteration, by the relevant parts of the law. But this sort of certainty is like the certainty that prevails in a family where a father answers his little son's question about where Port Darwin is by saying "in America," and then reacts to the son's fetching the world atlas and saying, "but Daddy, Port Darwin's in Australia," by giving him a thrashing.

This ideal of certainty about what the law says, a certainty brought about otherwise than through justice, is however in itself one of the most important causes of that *mentality* which so greatly repels unprejudiced people and which leads to a gen-

---

[2] *Reichsgericht* of 19 September, 1918, 100; von Hippel, ibid., 21.

[3] Radbruch, *Einführung in die Rechtswissenschaft*, 7th and 8th editions, 211.

eral contempt for lawyers as people. For if someone has really (that is, so as to deeply feel it) absorbed the principle that "the lawyer is the servant of form, not of the substance of justice,"[4] i.e., if he has become accustomed to place form above content, certainty about what the law says above justice, then he has become *slavish*, and will indiscriminately submit to *any* master. He will, with the apparatus for thinking in which he has been schooled by lawyerly technique, be at the disposal of the state power currently prevailing, the power that promulgates laws, just or unjust, and that also has the power to enforce them—quite irrespective of whether this state power brings weal or woe to its own people or to humanity at large.

Where was there ever a regime that did not have a host of lawyers at its disposal, to help it, as it were, to "legalize" itself? The same lawyers who served the revolutionary republic in France later worked for the Emperor Napoleon in order to create his *code civil* and to put it into practice. But even when Louis XVIII was restored to the throne there was no lack of compliant lawyers who supported *his* rule by means of law just as Napoleon's rule had earlier been supported, and just as, before that, the mob's and the demagogues' reign of terror had been represented as lawful and been advocated for by means of legal concepts. One might truly say: only lay your hands on power, on people who can construct a legal basis for your power, and you will never lack for anything! Hard and unbending in petty matters, in formalities; spineless and servile with respect to great matters, with respect to what is essential—this is how a lawyer who is a product of a law that has emancipated itself from an ethics that is itself without religion is shown to be in the light of day.

Of course we are not talking about *all* lawyers here, perhaps

---

[4] Ibid., 210.

not even about most of them, since the *atmosphere* in which many lawyers work is still influenced by the past, with its ethical and religious approach. And for this reason there are still, in all countries, numerous exceptions among lawyers. It is rather a question of the *type* that has made a decisive impression upon the lay world outside, and that has curtailed the respect once due to jurisprudence.

How different is the picture of the legal scholar sketched by Ulpian in his *Digest* (i, i, i) of the *Corpus Juris*!:

> Whoever wishes to concern himself with law must first know whence the name "law" is derived. It comes from justice; for law is, as Celsus has finely expressed it, the art of the good and the equitable. Therefore we may be called priests, since we cultivate justice and profess the knowledge of the good and the equitable, separating the equitable from the inequitable, and what is permitted from what is prohibited, seeking to make men good not only through the fear of punishment, but also by encouraging them to win the prize of honor, and seeking thereby, if I am not mistaken, a true, not an illusory philosophy.

If we compare this ancient conception of the lawyer's duty with the modern conception discussed above ("the lawyer is the servant of form, not of the substance of justice"), we notice the degradation to which jurisprudence has been subjected.

If, however, we ask ourselves what is the real reason for this degradation, this leads us to the fact of the "Fall" indicated earlier, that is, to the fact that jurisprudence, faced with the choice between *moral* and *mechanical* thinking (whose representatives, among others, were Goethe and Newton) *opted for mechanical thinking*. Or, to express the same thought in other words and with the help of a warning voice from the middle of the nineteenth century:

The false independence of the jurists, which was taken for scholarly progress, has not only distorted the theory of law, but has, in life, too, stripped law of its dignity, has promoted the idea of law as a mechanism, and has deprived legal concepts of their soul.[5]

[5] Adolf Trendelenburg, "Naturrecht auf dem Grunde der Ethik"(1860), 20.

II

The Nature of
True Jurisprudence

The Nature of the
Task of the True Jurist

G IVEN THAT the gradual obscuring of principled thinking in jurisprudence indicated above has taken place,
and, given that, as a consequence, there has been a
corresponding degradation of moral meaning of jurisprudence
for the world, this very fact faces us with the question how
jurisprudence is to inhabit the world according to its own true
nature and true vocation, or even how it might be rescued
from degencration and collapse. We need now, therefore, to
reconstruct the shape of jurisprudence as it might have been,
had this process of degeneration not taken place—or even as it
might be, were lawyers once again to become "priests of justice." For the inner disposition of the latter is especially relevant here. It is a question of the disposition that first makes a
legal scholar into a legal expert. What, then, is the inner disposition a lawyer must have in order to live up to his vocation in
the world?

From the example of legislative activity it can be especially
clearly seen what inner logic a person must satisfy when,
instead of merely taking up the existing law to study it, or to
interpret and apply it, he has ascended to the highest level of
responsibility and ability—the level of *making* law. In the *legislator* we find the highest manifestation of the nature both of
jurisprudence and of the jurist. Once we understand the nature
of the capabilities and duties of the legislator, it will not be diffi-

cult to comprehend the comparatively less significant expressions of these capabilities and duties in other areas of legal life. For in the legislator we find concentrated what is also present in a more dispersed state in all the other areas of law, and what constitutes the nature of the *juridical as such*. For the juridical as such is a particular mental disposition, distinct from the scientific, the philosophical, or the religious.

A legislator must not, for example, be a simple *idealist*, who over-estimates human nature, or who leaves the things of this world to divine providence. He must not, either, be a mere *realist* or fact-man, since his task is not to let facts hold sway just as they are, but to *order* them as they *ought* to be. The legislator must in no way be an enthusiast or a cynic; he must instead be at once a realist and an idealist. For as a legislator he must precisely and thoroughly know the realm of facts that is to be ordered legally. Yet he must, on the other hand, have before him in an equally precise and clear way the spiritual and moral idea according to which the realm of facts in question is to be ordered. Only *after* looking at the real and the ideal together does a third element emerge—the *norm*, the law.

The norm, as the work of art created by the legislator, is the creative result of considering the factual and the spiritual together. The true legislator looks at the factual otherwise than he looks at the spiritual. In the realm of the factual he looks, that is, at the *evils* present in it or that *could be present in it*, and for whose prevention or overcoming a law is in the first place required. In the realm of the ideal, by contrast, he casts a propitious gaze, in order to catch sight of the opposite of these factual evils. He directs, therefore, his *evil-seeking* gaze towards the factual, and his *propitious gaze* towards the ideal. And the more he is capable of *both*, the more he is fitted to be a legislator.

The legislator's task is not limited, however, to the recognition of *present* evil in the realm of the factual. He must also foresee the *possibility* of all further evils in this domain, in order to be able to avert them. For this he must be in a position consciously to grasp all the forms of malevolence, guile, and negligence that are even possible in this domain, and to know *a priori* the effects they might possibly have. He must, in preparation for making laws, continually keep his eye on a person who combines a monstrously refined intelligence with a bestial malevolence—a person, that is, who is a satanic apparition. And when elaborating law he must orient himself towards *this* almost satanic power in human nature. The more capable of this he is, the less *naive* he will be.

Naivety is, in fact, a mortal sin for a legislator. The other mortal sin would arise if the legislator were to fail to balance the *distrust* with which he must look upon *one* side of human nature (a side that is indeed factually present) with a *conscious trust* for the other side of human nature. For the whole legal order, even if it is grounded in the rule of force, rests in the last analysis on trust in the good and true as it is revealed in human nature. *Quis custodiat custodes?* is an ancient question, which self-evidently contains its own answer. "Who shall supervise the supervisors?"—no one on earth, but, rather, an eye that sees into the inward life of each of them, and a voice that ought to sound within the inward soul of each one of them. *Knowing* and *conscience*[1] are, in the last analysis, the foundation upon which rest even the most positivistically constructed legal tendency, and the one protected by all conceivable instruments of power. What is there behind this fact but that a greater significance is, and indeed must be, ascribed to moral consciousness than to all the instruments of power furnished by weapons, prisons, jails, and gallows? Behind this lies the (voluntary or involuntary) admission that there is an order higher than the

---

[1] The German juxtaposes the related words *Wissen* and *Gewissen*, rendered here, at some cost, as knowlege and conscience. ED.

moral world-order of force and power—that is, that *order in the world comes from God.*

The legislator, therefore, has *four* tasks. He looks at the state of affairs that is to be ordered, and must understand the evils already present in it; to this end he looks upon the domain of divine order and finds, by comparison, the present evils. Then he looks upon the subhuman and satanic, in order to foresee new evils that might be possible in the future. Last of all he creates law on the basis of his knowledge of the facts, of trust in God's being at work within human beings and in the world, of distrust of satan's works within human beings and in the world—law as the result of the painstaking inquiry into the depths of the satanic and subhuman, and of the faithful upward look towards the divine and super-human. The true origination of a law in the consciousness of a true legislator might be summarized using the following diagram:

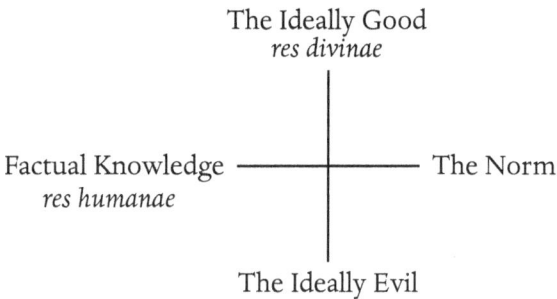

<pre>
                    The Ideally Good
                       res divinae

                          |
                          |
Factual Knowledge ————————+———————— The Norm
   res humanae |
                          |
                          |
                    The Ideally Evil
</pre>

The legislator is therefore the more complete the *higher* his gaze can travel up and the *lower* it can penetrate down. A legal genius is distinguished from a pettifogging lawyer by his ability to hold his consciousness in tension between this polarity, in a way that the latter simply cannot imagine doing. The thinking unfolded in this tension of consciousness between *good* and *evil* is, precisely, *moral* thinking, in contrast to *mechanical* thinking.

The latter can indeed serve these polar opposites, but it does not have them as the inward content of its consciousness.

Moral thinking, as the thinking that takes place in the categories of good and evil, is the source of law, and the ground upon which jurisprudence can and must rediscover its own true nature. We say "rediscover," because jurisprudence was once practiced in such a way as to be the discipline of the practical application of moral thinking to life.

For if we set up the diagram above so as to replace "factual knowledge" with *res humanae,* and "the ideally good" with *res divinae,* then we obtain the *first* stage of the emergence of the norm, and at the same time the first half of the formula for the idea of law in Justinian: "Juris prudentia est *divinarum* atque *humanarum* rerum *notitia. . . .*" We stand here at the point where the legislator *knows* (*notitia*) the domain of facts and compares it with the divine ideal. If however he extends the tension beyond the bounds of the *divine* and the *human,* so that the diabolic and sub-human is opposed to the *divine* and super-human, and that *knowledge* (*scientia*) results from this—then we get the second part of the formula from Justinian: *justi atque injusti scientia* [the science of justice and injustice]. Thus we rediscover the above formula for moral thought to be the foundation of jurisprudence in the *Corpus juris:*

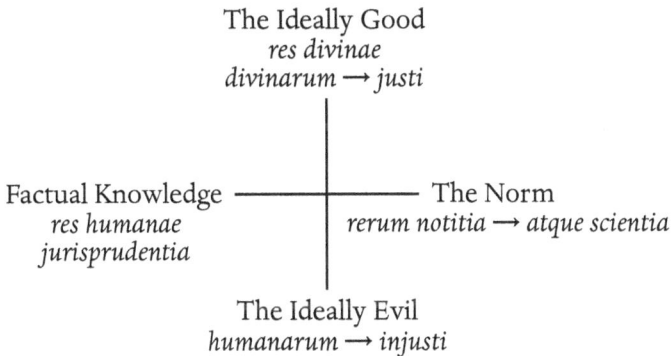

The Ideally Good
res divinae
divinarum → *justi*

Factual Knowledge ————————— The Norm
res humanae   *rerum notitia* → *atque scientia*
jurisprudentia

The Ideally Evil
humanarum → *injusti*

The path leads from *notitia* to *scientia*, from *familiarity* with the state of affairs to *certain knowledge* of the appropriate measures to be taken when thinking ascends from the empirical to the moral realm.

The Nature of True Creative Knowledge in the Cultivation of Jurisprudence

I N OUR PREVIOUS REMARKS we have repeatedly set out an opposition between quantitative and qualitative thinking, and between mechanical and moral thinking. Now we need to distinguish, as a matter of principle, the essential features of qualitative or moral thinking from that "pure thought" and "sensory intuition" which Kant held to be the sole sources of cognition. Plato had earlier pointed to a third source of cognition,[1] namely, *episteme* (a discernment creating adequate knowing) as against *dianoia* (knowledge on the basis of the logical inferences drawn from pure thinking) and *doxa* (mere opinion, grounded on sensory perception). These three kinds of knowledge form the bridge between the *moral* and the *natural* worldview. *Doxa* is the result of inferences from facts perceived by the senses; *dianoia* covers the middle region of pure thinking, where one concept is deduced from another; while *episteme*, finally, is based on an evidenced perception that is free from the senses, an immediate cognition of values grounded in the domain of the moral order of the world. Peter's profession of faith, illustrated in Luke 9:18–21, would, for example, in the

---

[1] Cf. Dr. J. Sauter, *Die philosophischen Grundlagen des Naturrechts* (Vienna, 1932), 23–24.

light of this Platonic division of the human capacity for knowledge, be understood as an ascent through three levels, from the mere *doxa* of the "people" to Peter's *episteme*, which came about not through the efforts of "flesh and blood" but as a "revelation from our Father in Heaven."

For in response to Christ's question, "Whom say the people that I am?" the disciples provide the mere *opinions* of the people: "John the Baptist; but some say, Elias; and others say, that one of the old prophets is risen again." None of these opinions is correct, since they are all based only on sensorily perceived *facts*. People read and heard about the prophets and about Elias, they heard and saw John the Baptist, and now they were trying to connect this new experience, that is, the appearance of Jesus Christ, with ideas familiar to them. The opinions of the people, their *doxa* are, in themselves, on the *way* to the truth, but they are incomplete, and thus do not constitute adequate knowledge.

From this first level follows the second, in the shape of the answer to the question Christ poses to the disciples themselves: "Who do *you* say that I am?" This question is put to *all* the disciples, and all the disciples were to give an answer to it. The answer Peter gave was not the answer of them *all* to the question, since Christ (according to Matthew 16:17) tells Peter, "Blessed art thou, Simon son of Jonah...," but does not say, "Blessed are you *all*, since you have collectively answered my question truthfully through the mouth of Peter." Consequently it is the *silence* of the disciples following upon this question which is their answer. Purely logical thinking, *dianoia*, is in and of itself incapable of achieving an insight into the *essence* of what is being asked about. It admits its incapacity by its silence. Conversely, this silence is the *best* human cognitive capacity can do in the circumstances. It does not block the path to the immediate knowledge that came about in Peter through the *third*, higher power, but leaves the way open for it.

Peter, therefore, could raise his voice before a circle of atten-
tive *listeners* and proclaim the words, "The Christ of God." *This*
reply is in no way a result of sensuous perception, any more
than of purely conceptual inference, but is instead the revelation of the immediate *discernment of value (episteme)* in Christ's
nature, as a manifestation of the moral world-order. *There,*
however, it is evident that Christ is no mere prophet, no mere
preparer of the way, but the very sun of the moral cosmos, a
sun that can all the more clearly be known since it outshines
with its light all other stars, just as the natural sun does in the
physical cosmos. It was this immediate vision of the moral cosmos, of the world of moral value (that is, of the "spiritual
world") that made it possible for Peter to achieve certainty
about "Christ as God." This is then also in another place (Matt.
16:17) expressly confirmed by Christ himself, when he says,
"Blessed art thou, Simon son of Jonah: for flesh and blood (i.e.,
the natural cosmos) hath not revealed it unto thee, but my
Father which is in heaven (i.e., in the moral cosmos)."

Here we have tried for the sake of clarity to illustrate the
immediate discernment of value (*episteme*) with the help of an
example borrowed from the realm of pure cognition of the
world, that is, from religion. But it can also be shown that a
similar, indeed essentially the same, discernment of value lies
at the basis of jurisprudence. In the first place, therefore, it is to
be shown that *law* is the basis of all jurisprudence, and that it is
in no way an object of sensory experience, nor can it be discovered in an empirical manner. For even if we acquire the *concept*
of law from individual legal phenomena, these phenomena
themselves only come about because there is law in the world,
law that reveals itself through these manifestations. The standpoint according to which appearances *conceal* their essence is to
be rejected, since it fruitlessly hampers knowledge. Appearances do not conceal their essence, or Kant's "thing-in-itself,"
but instead *reveal* it. The appearances of growth, for example,

do not conceal the growth of a tree, but reveal it. And a person's smile does not usually conceal his cheerfulness, but proclaims it. Just as we can think of a set of steps leading to the second floor either (if one is *negatively* disposed) as an obstacle that *divides* us from the second floor, or (if *positively* minded) as a means *connecting* us to the second floor, so we can think of every appearance either as an *obstacle* to knowledge, as something that *conceals* the essence of the object of knowledge, or as a *means* of knowledge, that is, as something that *reveals* the object.

The first standpoint could be illuminating only in the case of an inner aversion to and subjective rejection of those *difficulties in knowing* that the object brings with it: it is the standpoint which provides the justification *par excellence* for an "Ignorabimus" ("we shall never know"). If the "thing-in-itself" is unknowable because the shell of appearances concealing it is impenetrable, then we do not need to trouble ourselves about this "thing-in-itself," that is, about the essence of the thing and hence about true knowledge as such. We are justified, in such a case, in contenting ourselves with the *current* state of our capacities for knowledge and with a depth of insight into the world of appearances that corresponds to those capacities. Indeed, we even consider ourselves justified in setting up these limits—determined by our own capacities and the extent of our own appetite for knowledge—before *others*, as if these limits were the "limits of knowledge" as such; we think ourselves justified in permitting ourselves to describe anything others might have done by way of going beyond their own "limits," thanks to their greater effort, appetite for knowledge, or talent, as "indemonstrable" and "subjective," and to do away with their achievements as "audacious" and "presumptuous."

The second standpoint, by contrast, is to be treasured as something healthy and fruitful, since insofar as there has ever been or will ever be such a thing in the world as substantive progress in knowledge, such progress has always been and will always be owing to the faith that appearances have the positive value of revealing the essence of the thing, and that the modes of knowledge and capacity for knowledge currently available to us represent limits that can be *crossed*. "Seek, and ye shall find; knock, and it shall be opened" is also the moral foundation of any healthy and fruitful striving for knowledge.

With this, we profess our *realism*, in opposition to *nominalism*, and, indeed, in both the senses of this word: first, in the sense that ideas (*universalia*) are *realities*, which are not created by appearances, but which creatively determine appearances; and, second, in the sense that appearances are neither a delusion nor a covering over of the essence of the thing, but are rather *real* revelations of the *real* essence of the thing. Thus every sensory perception is, for us, of cognitive value, as every purely spiritual perception or intuition is also of cognitive value. In this, we connect the realism of medieval scholasticism, for which ideas were realities, with the realism that prizes *every* experience, as represented, for example, by Goethe.

For us the *universalia ante res* ("ideas are there before the appearances") are essentially identical with the *universalia in rebus* ("ideas are there in the appearances") that reveal themselves for *our knowledge* through appearances and that are grasped as concepts in the form of *universalia post res* ("ideas are there after the appearances"). Concepts are concepts of the ideas revealed in experience—this is roughly how we might formulate our idealist-empirical realism.

Correspondingly, we conceive of *law* too both as the *universalia ante res*, that is as the *a priori* spiritual reality that shapes the whole world of legal life as it appears, and also as the *universalia in rebus*, that is, as the inner driving force that is revealed in every phenomenon of legal life; and also, finally, as the *universalia post res*, the origin, essence, and content of the concepts that emerge in our minds on the basis of experience and intuition.

Law is therefore no mere "product of our culture," nor is it merely "praxis," or merely a "concept." It is a morally effica-cious spiritual reality, which both creates cultural values in the realm of universal culture and also appears as a concept in an individual's life of ideas and thoughts.

* * *

The reality of *law* is arrived at in three ways. Either we make ourselves familiar with the phenomena of positive law among various nations and in various epochs, and arrive from this at a *concept of law* which we acquire from these phenomena in their multiplicity. Or we examine universal life experience in the light of reason according to our best knowledge and our con-science—a life experience that includes both our own biogra-phy and that of humanity in general (i.e., world history)—and find that human life as a *whole*, in religion, science, art, busi-ness, politics, and the family, has to do with justice and injus-tice. Then law shows itself to be the principle of moral order in human life, as the shaping force of the life of culture; that is, we arrive at the *idea of law*. Or again, we direct our moral vision to the realm of what exists and what has been, that is, to the realm of the factual, and consider the creative spiritual ground of the world's existence with the question, "How *should* law be on earth, if it is completely to reveal its *true nature?*" When the gaze of moral thought is *immediately* turned upon the *true essence* of law, the divine essence of law as the highest spiritual and moral value is revealed. So the *ideal of law* is arrived at by inner intuition, just the idea of law is arrived at by putting expe-rience to use, and just as the concept of law is acquired by knowing the facts about positive law. The concept of law, the idea of law and the ideal of law belong together; they are three aspects of a *single reality*, and, at the same time, three levels of interiorization in the process of becoming conscious of this reality. And this is, indeed, the outcome of *doxa* in Plato's sense, that is, of the capacity to acquire the universal from particular phenomena: the *concept* of law, as law's *universale post res.* The outcome of *dianoia*, however, that is, of the capacity to cognize, by means of pure thinking, the influence of the ideal principle in the concretely particular, is the *idea* of law, as its *universale in rebus.* Finally, the outcome of *episteme*, as the capacity for immediate intuition of the spiritual and moral essence of values, is the *ideal* of law as its *universale ante res.*

These three levels of cognition of the nature of law belong unconditionally together. If even one of these levels is lacking or split off, it leads not only to incomprehensibility but also to atrophy. For if legal consciousness does not experience law as an *ideal* and as the highest value, it lacks moral seriousness and depth. If, on the other hand, legal consciousness gives up the *idea* of law as well, it loses its connection with human culture in general and its development in history—it falls out of the spiritual current of world history and becomes sectarian (e.g., national). And if legal consciousness loses even the *concept* of law, there is no such thing any longer as legal consciousness, but only an awareness of power and a glorification of force pure and simple. The dominant current of jurisprudence, however, took precisely this route of the loss of the higher levels of legal consciousness. The original unity of the levels of legal consciousness—divine law, human natural law, and positive law—was lost. In consequence, the consciousness of *divine law,* that is, the *ideal* of law, was the first to darken. Later the consciousness of *natural law,* that is, the *idea* of law, was pushed into the background. And at last even the *concept* of law itself was replaced in positive law by the *concept* of *power.*

This is how pure positivism emerged: a tendency lacking both ideal and idea, and possessing a falsified concept of law. A true awareness of law, however, results from *three* kinds of knowledge and represents the unity of the *three* levels of legal consciousness. These three levels essentially correspond to the concepts of "divine law" (*ius divinum* or *lex divina*), "natural law" (*ius naturae* or *lex naturalis*), and "positive law" (*ius humanum* or *positivum*). The battle that was waged in the nineteenth century between natural law and positive law (divine law, even as early as this, was already left out and left to the Catholics—and thereby dismissed) would never really have been able to take place if the philosophy of law and legal scholarship had remained sound, that is, if a split had not come about within the interaction of the different levels of legal consciousness. The debate mentioned remained unsettled, and natural law can still be championed. It faces, however, a more difficult situation than it faced during the period of the polemical battle: it is, to a large extent, no longer bothered with. It is as silent as the grave and is on the point of being forgotten.

This dead silence is, however, in itself a sign that there is a wish to be *freed* from law as a binding and superordinate value; it is more comfortable not to be so greatly obligated. For law in its true sense, that is, law as concept, idea, and ideal, exerts a morally obligating effect. To be a *guardian of the law*, when the law is conceived of in this way, is something quite different from being a guardian of a "law" that is the sum total of the statutes of whoever is currently in power. In the first case it means standing for an ideal, a historical legacy, and a well-grounded and clear discipline of thinking. In the second, however, it means standing only for the relative value of the current regime and the will of those in power within it. Pure power seems for many, however, to have a greater attraction than the law as an obligation to unconditional justice.

What then is the content, not of a law that is atrophied and obscured, but of a law that is *complete*, as a reality in the world, in culture, and in the consciousness of an individual?

The complete conception of law is based on discerning that, in the first place, the world is an *ordered* whole; that, second, this world order is a *moral* one; and, third, that human beings are called to order their own lives, using their creative powers in such a way as to *accord* with the moral world order. *Episteme*, the immediate perception of the *moral world order*, lies at the basis of the awareness of right and wrong. Only in this way can the freely assenting subordination of will-power to *laws* be explained and justified. It is the authority of the moral force that orders the world—that is, God's authority—which lends law its authority over arbitrary will. For our purposes it is irrelevant whether humanity first came to recognize this authority through an immediate discernment on the part of reason and conscience, or through a *reductio ad absurdum*, that is, by force of catastrophic experience—or, indeed, in both these ways. For us what matters is only the fact that humanity has recognized a binding principle, a *lex*, since the earliest times, and that the authority of law was derived from a cosmic dispensation.

What logic requires—that only something superordinate can possess authority, and that, consequently, humans can only be subordinate to something super-human, i.e., divine—is also confirmed by the facts of world history. Law-giving was connected with religion among all the peoples of the ancient world, and it was the priests and priestly orders who originally proclaimed the law. "Law" (in, for example, the Old Testament, or in the Avesta, or in the Law of Manu) originally meant the same as "divinely willed order," and a *righteous man* was a person who lived according to the law, who, that is, obeyed the commands and prohibitions of the will of God as made known in the law. Justice in the state was, therefore, seen as an expression of the true *order*, and Plato understood the virtue of justice as an expression of a person's truly *ordered* inner life. For in order to be *just*, wisdom, spirit, and temperance[2] must be present. A fool cannot be just, because he cannot judge, any

---

[2] Sophia, Andreia, Sophrosyne.

more than the coward can, for the coward's judgements are determined by fear. Nor, by the same token, can whoever lacks temperance be just, because he allows his passions and emotions to influence his judgements. *Justice*, therefore, as an internal order within the individual person, is the harmonious result of three virtues, virtues of thinking, of feeling, and of willing; just as *law*, as an external ordering of mankind, is the harmonious result of three areas of culture: religion, science, and politics. That is to say, law has the same ordering significance for the community as justice has for the individual person.

If in its deepest *essence* (that is, as an *ideal*) law is the intuition (*episteme*) of the moral world order, its *effect* consists in ordering human community so as to promote justice. This is the content of the *idea* of law. That this content will be moral goes without saying, since its inner nature (that is, the ideal in which this idea is rooted) is religious. Either the idea of law has no content at all (that is, nothing comes to mind when we say the words "idea of law"), or we conceive of it as having a moral content, specifically that of a justice that orders human society. If we *do* possess an idea of law, then we also possesses its moral content. Otherwise we have absolutely no idea of law at all, as, for example if we see in it a mechanical content borrowed, say, from physics, such as "the equilibrium and adjustment of particular interests."

Human language irrefutably testifies to the inner connection between law and ethical life. Moral and legal concepts are in all languages expressed either by the same word or by words derived from the same root. Russian *dolg'* (duty), like Latin *debitum* (from which we have French *devoir* and English *duty*), as well as German *Schuld* and *Schuldigkeit* (fault, guilt, debt), all have both a moral and a legal meaning; *dike* and *dikaiosyne*, *ius* and *iustitia*, like the Russian *pravo* (law) and *pravda* (justice, truth), the German *Recht* (law) and *Gerechtigkeit* (justice), and

the English *right* and *righteousness*, distinguish the two mean-
ings only through suffixes (compare also Hebrew *zédeck* and
zedukå).³ All that the genius of national languages does is to
confirm the fact that law is justice ordering the life of the
human community.

In the practice of the life of law, in legislation, for example, it
is a question only of that degree of justice which can *reasonably
be expected of everyone*. This degree of justice is the content of
the *concept* of law, which is acquired from the *phenomena* of positive law.

How is this degree specified, and what is the specific content
of the concept of law that results from the determination of the
degree of justice which can reasonably be expected of everyone?

Apart from the conditions the *legislator* must meet, that is,
that he be legitimately *authorized* with respect to those who are
to be subject to the law as well as with respect to the law as
such, every positive law must meet the following conditions.⁴

Substantively, every law must (1) be *just*. The *justice* of a law,
however, incorporates two further conditions:

(a) it must not contradict any *higher* obligation;⁵

(b) it must be either necessary or useful to the common
good.

---

³ Vladimir Solovyov, *Pravo i Nravstvennost* (Law and Ethical Life) [1897],
Complete Works (St. Petersburg, 1914), vol. 8, 539–40.

⁴ In our discussion of the conditions which every article of positive law
must meet, we follow the ideas of Theodor Meyer, S.J., in his outstanding
Institutiones Juris Naturalis (written in Latin): second edition (1906), Part 1,
263 ff.

⁵ "Every humanly decreed law contains within itself the essence of law
to the extent that it is deduced from natural law. If, however, it disagrees
with natural law in any particular, it is not a law, but the corruption of law."
S. Thomas Aquinas, *Summa Theologica* 1a2ae, q. 95, a. 2.

Every law must also (2) be *possible*, and indeed both *physically* and *morally* possible. *Morally*, a law is only possible if the requirements it presents to the current state of development of humanity in general do not demand more than such a humanity is capable of. The bar for what it is reasonable to expect can be set at variable heights among differing nations and in different ages according to the general level of culture in those epochs and places. In Plato's time, for example, it could not reasonably have been expected that slavery be abolished, and so legislation to this effect would have been *just*, but not *possible*. The case was the same in the thirteenth century, when Thomas Aquinas wrote on slavery. As is well known, he considered it lawful.[6] So what it is reasonable to expect is a *relative* quantity, which depends on the cultural relationships currently pertaining. Hence whoever holds merely to the concept of law, without thinking about the idea or the ideal of law, will necessarily become relativistic, even if he still has a concept of law and has not replaced it with the fetish of power. This is just what happened to a whole series of clear-headed thinkers, such as for example Gustav Radbruch, Georg Jellinek, Max Weber, Kantorowicz, Somlo, Böttger.[7] In their works it is a matter of investigating, from the point of view of jurisprudence and the philosophy of law, the various legal purposes pursued by individual (e.g., political) tendencies, and of setting out the results as knowledge, without any professed judgement on the scholar's own part.[8] Even though the inner attitude of this relativism is, in the last analysis, a "let each find his own way to salvation," it is the best thing (indeed the only thing) that can be

---

[6] *Summa Theol.* 2.2. q. 57, a3.

[7] G. Radbruch, *Einführung in die Rechtswissenschaft*; id. *Grundzüge der Rechtsphilosophie*; G. Jellinek, *Allgemeine Staatslehre* (3rd edition, 1924) and other works.

[8] Cf. G. Radbruch, *Grundzüge der Rechtsphilosophie*, 24–28.

hoped for when one only refers to a third of the complete range of legal consciousness: that is, when the two higher levels of legal consciousness are lacking.

* * *

What then is the content (the *ti esti*) of the concept of law, which remains fixed amid the tide of relativity?

First of all, the concept of law determines the relation between *persons*. Whatever is not a person, cannot be subject to law. Things have no rights. If I say, "I have rights," what I am saying at the same time is, "I am a person." A person, however, stands in contrast to a thing. A person is an essence that is not exhausted in its relation to another essence, which, that is, cannot, by its very essence, be conceived of as a mere instrument for another essence, but which is a goal and a purpose in and for itself. It cannot be penetrated nor made away with by another essence. Now, this signifies *freedom* in the true sense of this word, that is, not in the sense of a *liberum arbitrium indifferentiae* ("free choice among arbitrary points of view"), but, on the contrary, in the sense of a completely originary personal quality.

The concept of law therefore contains, as a quality of personhood, the concept of freedom, since there follows from the capacity for freedom a requirement for *independence*, that is, the recognition of our freedom on the part of others—which is precisely what the concept of law expresses. If I limit the expression of my freedom by recognizing the freedom of the other person to be just as much a matter of principle as is my own, or if, in other words, I recognize the other as a person, then I thereby obligate the other to recognize my freedom also; or, that is, *I turn freedom into law.*[9] My freedom as law,

---

[9] Or "into a right," the German here (and frequenctly in what follows) being *Recht*, which carries the meaning of both law and right, so that the translation will vary according to the relevant sense and emphasis. ED.

rather than merely as force, is thereby immediately dependent on the recognition of the *same* right of all other people. So the fundamental definition of the concept of law, or right, is as follows: *law is freedom upon the condition of equality.*[10] Since, however, the individualistic principle of freedom and the social principle of equality that limits it are opposites, it can also be said that the concept of law is *the synthesis of freedom and equality.*[11]

*   *   *

Solovyov's definition of the concept of law is entirely satisfactory when considering *private law,* but it shows itself to be incomplete when we start to think about *public law.* What underlies the definition given above is only one thing's being placed *next* to another, a coordination along a horizontal plane. This is just the conception which lies at the basis of *civil law.* But the matter stands otherwise in *public law,* where it is a question of one thing's being placed *over* another, of a vertical ranking. For this reason public law cannot be conceived of merely as the universal reciprocal recognition of freedom, since to its essence belongs also the *duty* to act or to refrain from acting, to the end of protecting and nurturing values that lie altogether outside the domain of the free disposal of the individual. This is how what is *sacred* (religion, the cultic, or *res sacrae*) are protected in *civilized states*—and it is to be hoped that this will continue to be the case.[12] Here it is not a question of the right of a person to

[10] This definition is given by the Russian thinker Vladimir Solovyov, whose argument we are for the most part following in defining the concept of law. *Pravo i Nravstvennost* ["Law and Ethical Life"], *Collected Works,* vol. 8 (1913), 530ff.

[11] Ibid., 532.

[12] States in which state-protected processions of the "atheist movement" are instituted for the purpose of making what is sacred ridiculous, and of desecrating it, may not be regarded as civilized states.

act freely, but of the protection of a *value* towards which we have duties precisely because of what is *valuable* in it. We have, that is, the duty to act in certain ways and to refrain from acting in certain other ways. Laws concerning the sacred, which were once (in the Middle Ages) so extensive, have today been condensed into paragraphs 166[13] and 366[14] of the German penal code. But they nevertheless remain in place and testify to the fact that duties exist not only towards other *persons*, but also towards *spiritual values,* which are nobody's "property."

Not only what is divine, but also what is human can be understood as a value and can, as such, obligate us. For example, the prohibition upon indecent behavior with animals (*Staatliches Gesetzbuch*, §175) cannot really be explained through the principles of civil law alone. For according to these principles an animal is a "thing" with which the proprietor can do as he wishes (for "property is the unlimited power of disposal over a thing"), provided he causes no harm to the interests of others. Now it is obvious that in the case of indecency with animals no sort of civil legal right held by another can be infringed upon: the action, indeed, remains strictly within the limits of the law of property. The fact that it came to be prohibited by a public law can only be explained by the fact that it is a question of the protection of an *ethical* value, that is, of the protection of

---

[13] "Whoever gives offence by publicly blaspheming against God with contemptuous expressions, or publicly mocks one of the Christian churches or any other religious society that has the right to exist within the Imperial Realm (*Reichsgebiet*), or mocks its institutions or rites, as also whoever causes public disorder of a contemptuous kind in a church or in another place dedicated to religious gatherings, will be punished by imprisonment for up to three years." Paragraph 167, by contrast, is a provision that protects the freedom of religion, but not a provision that protects religion as a *value.*

[14] "Whoever acts in contravention of the ordinances against the disruption of Sundays and feast days."

human dignity and the nobility of the human race. As well as protecting values that stand higher than humankind and values of a purely human kind, however, public law can also protect values that stand *lower* than what is human. Thus, for example, the prohibition on cruelty to animals (the *Tierschutzgesetz*[15] of November 24, 1933, or December 23, 1919)[16] protects unreasoning creatures from human coercion.

Thus it belongs among the tasks of public law, in addition to protecting the person and his or her rights, not only to protect values that rank higher than and equal with that of the person, but also, in some cases, those that rank lower. It can therefore be said, in the old (and clear) manner of putting this, that *God, Man,* and *Nature* are the objects of public law, whereas the object of private law is specifically *people's relations with each other*.

The content of the concept of law, therefore, can be given in the form of the figure of a cross, in which the vertical axis represents public law, and the horizontal axis, private law.

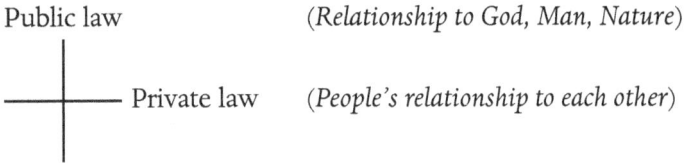

Public law   (*Relationship to God, Man, Nature*)

—————— Private law   (*People's relationship to each other*)

Now, since the definition offered above concerns only the horizontal line of this diagram, the definition must be completed by synthesizing the concept of law resulting from positive private law with the concept of law taken from positive public law. Such a synthesis would produce something like the following formula:

---

[15] "Animal protection law."
[16] §1. "It is forbidden to torment or mistreat an animal unnecessarily."

Law is freedom conditioned by equality and by obligations, which bring with them universally recognized spiritual and other values.

The concept of law acquired in this fashion is that of the final stage of the intensification and compression of the world of values corresponding to "European-Christian" culture. It can be recognized when its component parts are deepened and expanded. Just as steam becomes water when it cools, and just as water through further cooling becomes ice, so does the ideal of law, through the "cooling" of its moral and religious content, become the idea of law, which, through the further "cooling" (i.e., intellectualization) of its moral content becomes the concept of law.

This is the path we have followed. We began with the religious and moral; then we moved to the moral and intellectual; finally we arrived at the intellectual and phenomenal. We can, however, travel back along the same path. Through a *deeper* immersion in what the concept of law implicitly and explicitly contains, we can regain those summits of the moral and religious from which we earlier descended. The meaning of this for us would be that of a *method of completion*, that is, a method of *creating* the fundamental concepts concerning the value of legal life and the accountability of the concepts thus created. We would then have the *full circle* of different levels of thinking: juristic thinking, the philosophy of law, and the philosophy of religion—both in a descending direction, from the noumenal to the phenomenal, and in an ascending direction, from the phenomenal to the noumenal.

The second half of this path begins by anticipating that the above formulation of the concept of law will be interpreted in the same way as are, for example, wills in the civil code: "In the interpretation of a will, the actual wishes of the testator are to be sought, rather than sticking to a literal interpretation of what was written" (*Bürgerliches Gesetzbuch*, §133). This permission not to "stick to a literal interpretation of what is written" is the peculiar property of *juristic* thinking, which, by taking into account the particular circumstances of the case, good faith, usual practice, and the actions taken, aims to discover the *actual wishes* of the testator. *Behind* what is immediately manifest, juristic thinking seeks the "invisible" element, the actual wish of the testator, which is made known in these manifestations. If, however, we ask not only about this actual wish but also about the actual *content* (that is, apart from what is done in practice), then juristic thinking becomes philosophy of law; and if we ask about the moral nature, that is, about the *value* of this content, then philosophy of law becomes religio-philosophical thinking—until, finally, it comes to a halt in the pure intuition of *true essence*. These are the levels of thinking that correspond to the different levels of jurisprudence. The path runs from phenomena to concepts, from concepts to ideas, and from ideas to the ideal in which essence can be contemplated.

We make our start, however, with juristic thinking as a point of departure, that is, with the investigation of the will (i.e., the actual *opinion*, the *doxa*) expressed in this legal-conceptual formulation, "without sticking to the literal sense of what is written."

* * *

The concept of law as formulated above is the synthesis of polar opposites: *freedom*, as the thesis, and *obligation*, as its antithesis. And so, let us first examine the actual content of the word, concept, idea, and ideal of freedom.

In ordinary usage, "freedom" means the same thing as the absence of compulsion. Anyone who acts without being compelled thereto is free. Further, compulsion may come either from the world outside, or take its origin in the make-up of the person who is acting—for example, as concerns the latter, in the movements made by an epileptic, or the actions of a person who is mentally ill. For so long as they are subject to illness, the epileptic and the mentally ill person do not act freely. The epileptic does not put his will into effect at all; he is *compelled* by his seizure to perform the mechanical, spasmodic movements characteristic of his condition. In contrast to this, the mentally ill person does indeed put his will into effect, for he can will what he is doing; but he does not *know* what he is doing. Consequently, freedom requires not only the uncoerced activation of the will, but also that that will be *conscious*. What constitutes the juridical concept of freedom is the capacity consciously to put one's will into effect without compulsion. Therefore only that kind of illegal action which is *culpable*, that is, where the doer has *freely* perpetrated the deed, is punishable by law. The only kind of deed that counts as free is one where there has been intent, which is to say knowledge and volition of the outcome, or else negligence, i.e., where it was possible and obligatory to know about the outcome.

The idea of *free will* is the basis of all German law. It is the foundation of penal law, in which it alone renders the concept of culpability possible or thinkable; it is likewise the foundation of private law, and shapes all legal transactions (contracts, possessions). Even obligations under administrative law presuppose the freedom of the will, while the whole edifice of the Weimar constitution rested on the thoughts of the free citizen, that is, of a person endowed with a free will. One might therefore say that if faith in free will fails, the entire edifice of positive law—indeed the entire edifice of jurisprudence as such—falls with it.

Today, however, *determinism* has, with the growing influence of the natural sciences, become extremely widespread. According to determinism, the will is not free, since it is *determined* on one hand by the organism itself, and on the other by influences originating in the world of experience. In this view, the organism, which is the combined result of a long series of inherited characteristics and of the influences of sensory experience (e.g., education), completely determines the will; and likewise, the experience people have of being free when they make a choice is an illusion of the same sort as that of the sun's apparent movement around the earth. Biological materialism, as for example among the adherents of the theory of *Blood und Soil*,[17] cannot be other than deterministic. Adherents of such theories are also deterministic in practice; the Nuremberg laws of 1935 are both in their wording and in their spirit an expression of determinism. The penal law of the Third Reich, too, in which it is not the deed but the doer, the *criminal type*, who is subject to punishment and who is to be made harmless to the national community in various ways, even through castration for example,[18] is, precisely, determinism in practice.

It is therefore of the highest importance for jurisprudence and for the practice of law to answer the question whether human beings are free or whether determinism is valid. To answer this question, we have, again, to take account of the fact that *freedom* does not mean the capacity to wish for "whatever one likes," but that it is a question of a particular relation of *willing* and *thinking*. My freedom does not consist in my being able to will "whatever I like," but in my being conscious of what I am willing and what I am doing. The will in itself, that is, a will without the light of thinking to illuminate and guide it, is dark. In such a case we could not speak of a *free will* but only of a *free instinct*. If in my thinking I consciously propose to myself a clear goal and then strive to attain it through the exertions of the will appropriate thereto, I can indeed in such a case speak of freedom.

My will is free if it carries out what follows from my own thoughts, rather than from alien thoughts opaque and unfamiliar to me. A profound account of the problem of freedom in

---

[17] *Blut und Boden* was a Nazi-period slogan for nativist ideology.—Tr.
[18] *Staatliches Gesetzbuch*, §42 k.

this sense is contained in Rudolf Steiner's *Philosophie der Freiheit* (1894). We also meet this conception of freedom in the gospel. For when the crucified Christ says, "Father, forgive them, for *they know not what they do*," it is thereby stated that Christ's executioners are not fully responsible for their actions because they are not fully conscious of what they are doing, that is, they are *not* acting *freely*. Only *consciousness* produces freedom: "ye shall know the truth, and the truth shall make you free."

Jurisprudence, philosophy, and religion are therefore in agreement with respect to the problem of freedom. Each of them individually, and all three together, reject the standpoint of determinism. For jurisprudence, as well as for the philosophy of law, just as for religion, the fact of the freedom of the human person is the *keystone* that supports the whole edifice. The possibility of *morality*, meanwhile, is completely dependent on the presence of the freedom of the person. Were freedom not present as the fundamental presupposition of morality, the concepts of guilt and innocence, of sin and merit, even of good and evil, must needs be effaced from human consciousness.

* * *

The *essence* of freedom is the participation of the individual in the divine nature. Man is made in the image and likeness of God, that is, he is gifted with the creativity of the creator, the capacity to imprint what is most inward in him on the world outside. Man *can* realize his ideas through deeds. Experience teaches us this with complete certainty. No one can claim that, for example, Goethe wrote his *Faust* under the compulsion of external relations, or as a result of his inherited characteristics. The creation of *Faust* was a *free* act, an expression of the freedom that belongs to the essence of human personhood. What goes for *Faust*, however, goes, accordingly, for every human act in which a person shapes the outside world starting from his own consciousness.

71

The *essence* of freedom, that is, the *ideal* of freedom, is the divine creative spark man carries within himself as the "image and likeness" of the creator. The *meaning* of freedom in the world of values, that is, the *idea* of freedom, lies in the fact that this idea is presupposed by all human creativity, that is, by *culture*, in religion, art, morality, and the legal system. The *concept* of freedom for the practice of the legal system consists in the relation between knowing and willing, in which a person *knows* what he is *doing*. As a *reality*, however, that is, as the totality made up by the concept, idea, and ideal, freedom represents a *value*, for which it is worth living and dying. And this value of freedom, with all its moral and religious depth, lies at the core of jurisprudence, not only as its presupposition, but also as the object which jurisprudence exists to protect.

If we once see this fact, and value it as we really ought, then we become *serious* practitioners of jurisprudence as the nurse and protectress of human freedom, which freedom is the foundation of all true culture and an aboriginal gift of God. In this way Ulpian's expression in the *Digest, cuius merito quis nos sacerdotes appellet* ("by virtue of which one might describe us [jurists] as priests"), will once again become true, and the standing and respectedness of jurisprudence in the world will be restored again!

* * *

Now, if the concept of freedom is in this way treated as sacred, another cultural value will, as a consequence, also be sacralized—the value of *property*. For in order for us to be able to exercise our freedom, a domain in the outside world must be assigned and guaranteed to us in which we can do this unconstrictedly. This domain is, precisely, property.

If property, juridically, means *immediate lordship over a thing*, it is simultaneously a foundational value for the philosophical conception of culture as the necessary domain for the *exercise* of freedom, and is also one of the foundations of religious ethics. For how could I ever obey the gospel's demand that I should "to him that taketh away [my] cloke forbid not to take [my] coat also" (Luke 6:29), if neither cloak nor coat belongs to me, and if I therefore have no unlimited right to dispose of them as I wish? A soldier, for example, who does not own the uniform he is wearing, because it is army property, would never be able to act in this way. Only private property, in the sense of the most unlimited power of disposal possible, makes it possible to *give gifts* and to make sacrifices, and thereby makes possible the ethically sublime as such in the domain of material goods.

The meaning of property for religion is not, however, confined to property's moral value for the conduct of our life, but also reaches to cosmological heights. There it appears, in the Mosaic creation narrative of the fifth day of creation, as an inseparable companion of freedom: "And God said, Let us make man in our image, after our likeness: and let them have dominion over the fish of the sea, and over the fowl of the air, and over the cattle, and over all the earth, and over every creeping thing that creepeth upon the earth" (Gen. 1:26). The basic religious thought of this text is that we are endowed with freedom and that at the same time the whole realm of nature, in which to exercise that freedom, is given to us. With the birth of freedom, that is to say, the archetype of *property* is born also. The whole of nature is the property of man, who is endowed with freedom. *Freedom* as the image and likeness of the creator, and *property* as lordship over all "things" in nature, belong together from their very origin.

★ ★ ★

The pole opposite to freedom, which forms the other part of the synthesis of the concept of law, is *obligation*. Obligation belongs just as inwardly and indivisibly to the concept of law as does personal freedom. For simply the fact that I am not the only one who is free, but that others around me are free too, *obliges* me to respect them, that is, places limits on the exercise of my freedom. This, however, is only the *negative* side of obligation—that is, *not* to step beyond the boundaries of my own realm of freedom. This kind of obligation is *equality*. For there is no positive, qualitative equality: equality can, at the most, only be a degree of similarity. Its content is, for legal consciousness, limited to that of being a negative obligation *not* to treat others differently from the way in which I should like to be treated myself.

The relevance of obligation to the concept of law is not, however, confined to the obligating effects of equality. For as we already saw earlier (p. 64 ff.), there are *values* that obligate us through their existence and their very nature. We have already tried to illustrate, using some examples, the fact that these values can either rank higher than, the same as, or lower than, human beings. Public law protects these values; in a civilized state there are laws that protect spiritual and other values. Such protective legislation consists not only of penal laws aimed at preventing attacks upon the values protected, but also of laws making particular actions obligatory. The duty to undertake *military service* is, for example, a duty to *fight*, to protect real or supposed values—for example, to fight for the sovereign state. But it is not only state law that contains prohibitions and instructions, but also *church law*, which once outranked state law, and which was already flourishing in an age when none of the states currently constituted was in existence. The instruction of the Catholic Church to attend Mass on Sundays and on certain festal days is a pure command to positive action. The state's prescription of compulsory school attendance is a similar obligation to positive action.

Here, legislation goes beyond the limits of the aim of *protection*; it extends its aim to the *care* of particular values and takes it upon itself to give *guidance* as to this care. Law, here, becomes a guiding and obligating *straight line* towards a specific *goal*: in the case of the obligation to attend Mass, towards the goal of active participation in the *effects* of the Sacrifice of the Mass, and in the case of compulsory school attendance, towards the goal of attaining a specific level of *education*. The requirement for and care of specific universally recognized values, and the guidance given towards a value as a goal, belong likewise to law as statutes making particular actions obligatory. The *concept* of public legal obligation could, therefore, be outlined by saying that *obligation under public law protects, nurtures, and requires universally recognized values.*

⋆ ⋆ ⋆

Such an obligation, as discussed above, would however be impossible if there were no *cultural values* in the first place, if these values went unrecognized, or if there were not individual people authorized to protect, nurture, and require these values. This leads us to the idea of a hierarchically articulated *authority*, that is, both a ranking order of *values* and a ranking order of those who *embody* them.

If we follow the significance and effect of this idea in the history of humanity, we go from the level of the skilled laborer or specialist to that of the aristocrat, from the aristocrat to that of priestly kingship, and, finally, from priestly kingship to a pure *theocracy*. The value of all values is God, and the plenitude of grace in contact with Him; everything valuable in values derives from God, and the authority of all who administer these values derives in the last analysis from God. *Primordial governance*, that is, the highest and first law, is the divine law (*lex divina*), which is an expression of the wisdom of providence, and contains within it the whole plan of the creation—the *lex aeterna*.

Thus the first "publicly-legal" law must have come to be in the age and the way of thinking characterizing the primeval epoch, when there was a lived *contact* with the value of all values, that is to say with God. This epoch and this way of thinking is described by the Bible as "being in Paradise." And just as we found the origin of the essence of *freedom* and of *property* illustrated in the Mosaic book of Genesis, so do we find the origin of *obligation*, that is, the *first law*, in Genesis also:

> And the Lord God commanded the man, saying, Of every tree of the garden thou mayest freely eat: But of the tree of the knowledge of good and evil, thou shalt not eat of it: for in the day that thou eatest thereof, thou shalt surely die. (Gen. 2: 16–17)

Man was to be connected to and to participate in all the flows or currents connecting earth and heaven ("trees") and to take to himself ("eat") their effects ("fruit"); but he was to become acquainted with the flow of relation between spirit and nature (heaven and earth), which places spirit and nature in a relation of *opposition* (i.e., as "good and evil"), only through *intuition*, not through taking its effects ("fruit") into his own essence ("not eat"). Man is to experience and to know the opposition of good and evil *externally*, that is, outside his own essence, and is not to become himself the stage upon which this opposition plays out: for this last would import a tension and an abrading effect that leads to discord, sickness, and death.

This archetypal law lies, as a *fundamental obligation*, at the basis of all further and subsequent rational and legal obligations (laws). Man is to avoid whatever brings discord, sickness, destruction, and death, and to embrace whatever works to protect and nurture harmony between consciousness and nature, which is to say health, edification, and life. In other words, man is not inwardly to bind himself to the *destructive forces* of the world; these forces are not permitted to belong to the human realm. Man *ought*, on the other hand, inwardly to bind himself to the *constructive forces* of being, for to bring about what is creative and constructive is man's original vocation.

And in *this sense* humanity was first theocratically, then aristocratically governed, until finally it was governed by the reason of democratically chosen representatives and specialists through public legislation (*alongside* the guidance of the Church, which in principle retained its original *authority* and *hierarchy*).

★ ★ ★

Thus we have once more traced the path from the concept to the idea, and from the idea to the ideal, in order to illustrate a *method* of thinking that does not merely *separate* things, but distinguishes them and *connects* them in a unity. For jurisprudence has lost a great deal by falling victim to the tendency to *split* things off from each other. First it was separated from religion, but then it was separated from morality as well, as also from philosophy. Its individual domains, too (private law, penal law, administrative law, law of state, national law, church law, etc.) are on the point of becoming completely split off from each other. Jurisprudence owes the *essence* of its concepts, meanwhile, to religion, owes the *method* according to which these concepts are to be deployed to idealist philosophy, and owes the *application* of these concepts to a practice developed over the course of two and a half millennia, for more than two thousand years of which jurisprudence was part of an organic *whole*.

What have we gained by accepting as a governing direction the attempt to split, to separate things off from each other? Loss of the ideal, loss of the method for thinking in a morally principled way, the mechanization of concepts, and, as a result of these, superficiality, a lack of true seriousness. These are the fruits of the separation from the *ground* out of which jurisprudence has grown and from which it has created its vital forces and its own substance—and from which it must create these things anew, and even more extensively, if it is not to wither and to go to ruin.

The Goal of
a True Legal Policy

JURISPRUDENCE and the careful practice of the law—that is, legal "scholarship," the judiciary, and the legislature—exercise a shaping *influence* on the life of human civilization. It is the task of *legal policy* to ensure that this influence is directed towards a *goal*. Legal policy is the positing of a universal goal that is to be devised and kept to by the theory and practice of jurisprudence. It has to specify the *direction* to be taken by all of legal life.

The first and most important question for legal policy is therefore the question which goal it is to set itself: only when we are clear about what our goal is can we find the way to reach it.

Now the goal can be sought either in the requirements of a *worldview*, or in an approach that lacks any worldview and proceeds along *empirical* lines. In the first approach a goal is sought that is governed by the ideal set by the worldview from which we start out. In an approach without a worldview, conversely, we are looking for something whose nature is unknown, but is to be revealed by positive or negative *experience*.

As regards the empirical method, it is—as a way of setting a goal—to be decisively rejected. For in the first place, there is no such thing as a person quite without a worldview of some kind, whether conscious or unconscious; and in the second, even if there were such a person, how would he be able to *rec-*

ognize any goal that experience might show him as a goal? What criterion would he have for distinguishing the goal from the plenitude of experience in general? Could this, however, nevertheless be done, it would be done thanks either to pure caprice or to the presence of a principled criterion, that is, to the effect of a worldview. And if, despite all this, someone were to succeed in excluding alike *any* element of a worldview and any element of caprice, the empirical goal found would at the same time be the end, that is, *death*. For from a purely empirical point of view everything *ends* in its demise, in death. Death is the final empirical reality, and consequently the empirical goal of everything manifested in time.

It therefore only remains to seek the goal of legal policy in a worldview, that is, in an all-embracing knowledge governed by principles. A worldview, however, can in principle only be of one of two kinds. Either it considers the *world as such* or it considers the world as an *expression* of something higher than the world. That is, the world can only be either "observed" or "read." Just as, for example, a book can either be looked at as a phenomenon (that is, we can observe the number of pages and chapters, the kind of paper it is printed on, the nature of the ink, the letter forms used, and so on) or on the other hand be read as a book, so in the same way can the world either be looked at and investigated, or be looked at and known precisely as a world, that is, as the expression of the workings of the consciousness that created it.

In other words, the world can be conceived of either as God's creation, or as an automaton (or again, as an "organism" or as a "machine"). If the world is understood as an automaton, it is not really necessary to trouble about setting any further objective for it: what will happen will happen. The only human objectives still conceivable in such a world are either those of not-being, of some form of suicide, or else utilitarianism as represented by Jeremy Bentham (1748–1832), according to which "the greatest happiness of the greatest number" is to be striven for. Happiness as an end in itself, is not however a long-term objective; its content inevitably cannot be anything other than the social enjoyment of all the available pleasures of life. A sort of "social Epicureanism" in the sense of a *carpe diem* would in practice be the consequence of an ideal consisting of happiness alone.

The ideal of happiness, however, need not necessarily consist in earthly happiness alone. If we understand the world not as an automaton but as a creation, the ideal of happiness can be incorporated into a higher and more comprehensive ideal. Leibniz, for example, whose ideas of knowledge and substance are grounded in the unification of differing elements, in "harmony," unified utilitarianism with a theological and teleological conception of the world. Positing the perfection of the individual and the community as a goal, Leibniz distinguishes three levels of spiritual comportment with respect to this goal: (1) *utilitas*; (2) *humanitas*; (3) *religio*.

Each of these levels is higher than its predecessor. *Utilitas*, as the first level, corresponds to utilitarianism's ideal of happiness, but dignified and internalized by virtue of its relativity as a level preliminary to the other two. The level of *humanitas* has as its goal the community of free human personalities. To it corresponds the third part of the digest of legal prescriptions in Justinian's *Institutes*: *honeste vivere, alterum non laedere, suum cuique tribuere.*[1] The *suum cuique tribuere* ("grant everyone that which belongs to him") is the fundamental legal rule that corresponds to the level of humanity, while the rule *alterum non laedere* ("do not injure others")[2] applies to the level of utility. The third level of justice, however, which aims to realize the precept *honeste vivere*, strives towards the goal of the religious man, who lives

---

[1] Justinian, *Institutes*, 1.1, 3.

[2] Leibniz uses the formulation *neminem laedere*.

in concord with God as a *vir bonus*. To these three levels of justice correspond three levels of the natural community:

1. the community of the family;
2. the community of civil society; and
3. the community of religion,

where each of these communities corresponds to a level of law:

1. the *ius strictum* corresponds to the community of the family;
2. *aequitas* corresponds to the community of civil society;
3. *pietas* corresponds to the community of religion.[3]

At the first level, men live and strive for the realization of true happiness through individual perfection; at the second level they strive for shared perfection as a community; at the third level they live, as a community, in communion with God. In other words, the autonomous family ascends to the morally-grounded state, and the state attains its goal when it becomes a church, that is, when it becomes an organic community on a basis that is neither economic nor political, but religious.

It should be noticed here that Leibniz's final goal is not that the church should be absorbed into the state, but that the state should become a church. A "state church" would therefore be the complete opposite of Leibniz's conception. What hovers before him as the future goal to be striven for is not the gradual absorption of the church into the state, but the gradual absorption of the state, with its economic and political special interests, into the church. This would be the realization of the Augustinian *civitas Dei*.

Once one has decided in favor of the theological and teleological worldview, an abundance of valuable and useable

[3] J. Jacoby, *De Liebnitii studiis Aristotelicis*, 33–38.

thoughts, handed down from the past by minds such as Fransisco de Vitoria, Gabriel Vasquez, Hugo Grotius, and others, is available to anyone concerned with the teleology of law today. And just because of their abundance, one is compelled to choose, to adhere to, a *single* system of thought, one sufficiently capacious to stand as a *representative* of the perennial philosophy of the past. Leibniz meets this requirement to an extraordinary degree: as a jurist, as a philosopher, and as a historian, he covers the whole range of intellectual work which, from the age of Plato and Aristotle down to the eighteenth century, had been carried out in the fields of theology, philosophy, and jurisprudence. But the real reason we adhere to the intuitions of Leibniz here is that his intuitions seem to us to be fruitful and stimulating for the problem with which we are concerned. For even the extremely compressed account of his intuitions given above places us face to face with the central problem: towards which state of society are we to aim? According to Leibniz's principles, the answer would be as follows: what is to be aimed at is a *harmonious* state of society, that is, a state of society in which *all* levels of development can work together and alongside each other, while each level retains a pronounced tendency to move towards the levels above it. Society is, on the one hand, to be internally *plural*—for people are *not* all alike, when it is a question of the way in which they think—while on the other it is to be organized as a *unity*, since peace is to prevail among the different levels of humanity. A hierarchical social structure is to be linked with equality before the law in such a way that neither revolution nor tyrannous dictatorship is thinkable. Now, what would a specific state of society meeting these requirements be like?

★   ★   ★

A community comes into being and remains viable thanks to the common *value* whose bearer it knows itself to be. These values can be in the *past*, in which case it is a common tradition that binds people together in a community; they can be in the *present*, for example, particular institutions and ways of life; or they can lie in the *future*, when for example they are concerned with a state that has set itself a programmatic goal of expansion.[4] The Soviet Union, for example, has a political goal that reaches into the future; China, conversely, had for millennia the political goal of the conservation of the traditions of the past.[5] The Western democracies see it as their task to work in the *present* towards the end of the safeguarding and dissemination of the democratic system. There is *one* community, however, which has the goal simultaneously of nurturing tradition, of developing a universal efficacy in the present, and of striving towards a distant universal goal in the future—namely, the *Catholic Church*.

What distinguishes the Catholic Church is that it serves the goal of the conservation and nurture of tradition in a very intensive way, yet at the same time participates no less intensively to shape and contest all areas of contemporary life—and also strives towards an ideal of the future that embraces all mankind. Out of all known larger human communities, the Catholic Church is the most perfect in this respect: it never forgets the past, it works and takes care for the future, and it takes an active position towards the events of the present day. It is also the most solid and enduring community, not only in comparison to political communities, but also in comparison to states (apart from those of the Far East)—indeed, in comparison to nations themselves. It has outlived all crises: the struggle with pagan empire, the barbarian migratory invasions, the encounter with Islam, the Reformation, the French Revolution and the Napoleonic wars, the wave of materialism in the nine-

---

[4] Cf. G. Jellinek, *Allgemeine Staatslehre* (3rd edition, Berlin, 1920), 242ff.
[5] It is to be recalled that this book was written in 1944. ED.

teenth century, and finally, also, the storms of the present. In some of these crises, empires collapsed and dynasties rose and fell. Yet the Church remained standing and conserved its tradition, its hierarchy, its continuity, and its ideal. How is the fact of the super-eminence of the Catholic Church to all other human communities in this respect to be explained?

In my view, the reason lies in the fact that it is the Catholic Church which most corresponds to the requirements for a harmonious state of society as set out above. It is the most democratic community, since every son of a peasant can in principle achieve the highest station, the papacy. It is at the same time the most aristocratic community, since it is constructed in a strictly hierarchical fashion. It is arranged more plurally than any other community (one need only think of the many lay and monastic orders with their rules and regulations), yet at the same time displays a unity among all the different races and nations of the world, a unity that could never be attained or preserved by force, but could only be brought about, and will only be brought about, by virtue of a unity of values (of religious belief, for example).

Reason postulates the following, and the experience of the nineteenth century teaches us the same. If one wishes to bring about a durable, solidly based and harmonious community—that is, one that embodies *peace*—then either one must recognize that the Catholic Church is such a community, or, if for any reason one is unable or unwilling to recognize this fact, one must found another community that is in all essentials modeled on the Catholic Church: a community held together by a common ethico-religious ideal, by a common worldview, and by a common tradition, and which is nevertheless not national, nor confined to a single social class, but has a universally human character. Any attempt to form a community lacking these qualities will *eo ipso* be destined to collapse. To the extent that communities in part evince some of these qualities, however, they will be the more capable of possessing greater stability and permanence.

★ ★ ★

If we first of all draw out the *negative* implications of the declaration of principle given above, we find that:

(1) No *national* state, to the exent that it is merely national, can ever bring about the harmonious state of society that is to be striven for.

(2) No *class* state, to the extent that it takes the domination of a single class as the basis of its social system, can conceivably bring about a harmonious state of society.

(3) No *agonistic* state, that is, a state that is indifferent to any worldview (to the extent that this indifference is not a framework of tolerance but a dominant spiritual and social tendency) can bring about a harmonious state of society.

(4) And finally, no social system that has come about on the basis of *revolution*, to the exent that it erases tradition and interrupts cultural continuity, has a chance of establishing the "social system of peace."

The *positive* implications are as follows:

(1) Every international state, that is, every state in which a number of peoples are brought together, not as rulers and ruled, but through a commonly recognized cultural value, has the prospect of participating in the future organization of humanity towards a "harmonious state of society," insofar as something supra-national and humanly valuable is brought about in it.

(2) Every state in which the classes *work together*, even if only in part, instead of struggling against each other, is to this extent called to contribute to the future shaping of the human community.

(3) Every state that develops an active tolerance towards constructive and committed cultural life, a tolerance developing from the knowledge which that state has acquired as to the limits of what it can attain (for the state does not *produce* any positive cultural values, but can only favour and protect such values through external relationships) has a chance of being a useable *vessel* for the content of the future life of the community.

(4) And finally, every social system that nurtures the cultural heritage transmitted to it towards the end of progress and development is called to contribute to building a positive future.

*   *   *

The task of a legal policy is thus to realize a just social order, that is, to emancipate jurisprudence and the practice of law from their national limitations and restrictions, as well as from any favoring of an individual class at the expense of another; and it is also ever-intensifyingly and progressively to protect and demand those spiritual goods that bind humanity together in a common worldview and a common ideal on the path towards peace and freedom of belief.

This task can only conceivably be executed, however, if jurisprudence and the practice of law once again reach a level at which, free from the influence of aspirations to party-political power, national power, and state power, they will be in a position to devote themselves to the service of *humanity*, as a supranational branch of learning and a supra-national practice. This, however, brings us to the question of how a *regeneration* of jurisprudence is to be brought about.

III

Towards the Regeneration
of Jurisprudence

The Regeneration of Method

TWO TENDENCIES and two methods have stood in opposition to each other for almost two and a half centuries: the tendency and method of *realism*, for which the contents of thought and spiritual values are objective *realities*, and the tendency and method of *nominalism*, for which the "universalia," that is, universal concepts, are only words and have no import outside the subjective realm of thinking, since they describe nothing objectively real.

The first tendency originates in the temples of the mystery-cults of early antiquity and manifests itself thence in the daylight of the public realm, particularly with Thales (626–545 BC) and Heraclitus (c. 540–480 BC), Pythagoras (sixth century BC), and Empedocles (490–430 BC)—until it comes to fruition in Socrates (469–399 BC), Plato (428–348 BC), and Aristotle (384–322 BC). From Plato and Aristotle the history of realism continues through the Middle Ages, where it is especially represented by John Scotus Eriugena (ninth century AD), by the School of Chartres, by Albertus Magnus (1207–1280) and Thomas Aquinas (1225–1269), and on into the modern era, where it is championed by a number of thinkers, such as Leibniz (1646–1716), Wolff (1679–1714), Fichte (1762–1814), Schelling (1775–1859), and Hegel (1770–1831), who, however, are usually described as *idealists*.

The other tendency began with the Sophists (Protagoras, Gorgias, and others), came to fruition with the Cynics, and was revived in the Middle Ages by Roscelin of Compiègne. Condemned at the Council of Soissons in 1092, nominalism

nevertheless continued to have an influence, and was success-
fully defended by, in particular, Roger Bacon (1214–1294), and,
in the fourteenth century, William of Ockham (1270–1347).
From these sources, nominalism came—thanks to the successive efforts of Francis Bacon (1561–1626), Thomas Hobbes
(1588–1670), John Locke (1632–1704), and David Hume (1711–
1776)—to dominate in the field of natural science, and, in the
nineteenth century, it gradually won the upper hand, too, in
almost all aspects of Western academic thought.

Significant variations and differences in quality and overall
direction manifested themselves, of course, in the long course
of the development of, and struggle between, these two tendencies; but the thread that remains constant throughout all
these centuries, and that constitutes the real continuity of each
of these tendencies, remains the same. It is the relationship
each has to the content of thinking and spiritual values. This
relationship was and remains the same in each tradition.
Where the "realist" experiences a real illumination from the
light of *cosmic* consciousness, the "nominalist" finds nothing
but a humanly fashioned outline *description* for a collection of
similar experiences. Thus a "realist," for example, when he
places the concept "God" at the center of consciousness, can
experience and know, through this concept—just as through a
window—something *more*, which is contained *in* this concept,
and which is revealed *by means of* this concept. He can experience the *breath* of a spiritual efficacy, a stream of illumination
and deep rest that fills his being: for the concept "God" points
to the reality of God and binds us to that reality. Just as the
wind is a reality, because its breath breathes upon us when we
open the window, so too is God a reality, because his breath
penetrates inside me when I think the thought "God."

The capacity to have *a perceptible experience within* intellec-
tion is one that is peculiar to the "realists" as the bearers of a
specific type of human constitution. This capacity is lacking in

people disposed to nominalism. When, for example, a "nomi-nalist" concerns himself with the concept "God," it is for him only an *abstraction* from everything moral experienced in par-ticular instances of human life. It is therefore a *remnant* left over after all the specific traces of these manifestations have been erased. Then he can either "believe" in God, that is, recognize God as a being on pragmatic grounds (in the spirit of the prin-ciple *si Dieu n'existait pas, il faudrait l'inventer*),[1] or else *deny* Him on equally pragmatic grounds (as did Friedrich Nietzsche, for example). In both cases, that is, whether the existence of God is acknowledged or denied, the person disposed towards nomi-nalism remains unaffected by the *content* of the concept "God." His conduct is determined, both positively and negatively, by *other* grounds and motives to be found outside the content of this concept.

Any dispute among these two differently disposed types of people is condemned in advance to be fruitless, for it is not a question of their having differing opinions or points of view, nor merely of their drawing differing logical inferences, but of their being differently constituted. The "nominalist," who sees nothing *in* the concept but a generalization from ordinary experience, will always assert that the "realist" is projecting his own subjective feelings and imaginings into his thoughts, that he is not thinking rigorously. The "realist," by contrast, who finds an almost palpable reality in thought, a reality that is self-evident to him, will find his opponent guilty of superficiality and hastiness: if the nominalist had taken more trouble, rather than contenting himself with a superficial view of thought, he would have arrived, according to the realist, at the same per-ception as himself.

Now, in reality, it is not a case either of the realist's projecting his own feelings and imaginings into the concept, or of any

[1] "If God did not exist, it would be necessary to invent him."

superficial haste on the nominalist's part, but of the presence or absence of a quite specific ability. Just as there are color-blind and fully-sighted people, and just as there are musical and unmusical people, so are there also people who are "blind" to ideas and people who can "see" them. Nominalism is "idea-blindness," that is, it is an inability to perceive the qualitative and moral *life* of thoughts. To the nominalist, all thoughts are "colorless" and gray. The nominalist experiences thoughts as being without qualities; that is, he experiences thoughts merely formally and technically. The *materially* and morally efficacious aspect of concepts lies beyond his perceptual field.

And so we come back once more to the starting point of the whole present study, that is, to Goethe's argument with Newton as representing two different kinds of life for a thinker. Where Newton sees only quantities, Goethe sees qualities, and is perplexed that Newton and his disciples cannot see what is so completely clear to him. In just this dispute, it is Goethe's "realist" constitution that collides with the Newtonians' nominalism, and the conflict is irreconcilable for just this reason.

The practical consequences resulting from the fact of this difference in human dispositions are, however, as follows.

I

Jurisprudence is built on the foundation of the value of the idea of *law* and of the complex of ideas organically bound up with that idea. Anyone who wants to understand, practice, and develop jurisprudence *must* be in a position to recognize and to value its spiritual and moral foundations. A person who is "idea-blind" is, however, incapable of doing this, because for him there is *no* spiritual or moral foundation to jurisprudence, but only, say, a sociological, economic, or political foundation. Ideas and ideals belonging to *other* fields will therefore lie closer to his heart than *law in itself*, because, as a nominalist, he cannot know or recognize the latter.

If, therefore, one wishes to prevent the total demise of jurisprudence, or its perversion into the opposite of what it is and should be according to its own nature, the same thing must be as a matter of principle done for jurisprudence as has already been done for its neighbor discipline, theology. "Nominalists" do not belong in the field of theology, and the nominalist approach has been eccelesiastically "condemned"—has, that is, been excluded from the domain of theological instruction, on the grounds that it endangers the intellectual foundations of Christendom. This is absolutely consistent and correct, for how can certain people be called to represent particular spiritual values as realities, when they see those values not as realities, but only as *words*?

Now, the motives that determined these measures' being taken in theology are also applicable to the field of jurisprudence. For jurisprudence too, like theology, is grounded not upon *facts*, like natural science, but on *ideal* values. And anyone who has neither eye nor ear for these ideal values can just as little be a practitioner of jurisprudence as someone who is blind and deaf to the facts can be a natural scientist. Catholic theology saw this with complete clarity, and drew the necessary practical conclusions. It was able to do so because it was centrally administered.

Jurisprudence, however, which is split into national branches, and which is exposed to all manner of possible external influences, is self-evidently not in a position to protect itself by taking a single such measure. Yet it is possible for this insight to gain ever more ground—the insight that there can be no jurisprudence without *law*, and that people who are simply "idea-blind" are also blind to the law, and, consequently, can have no part to play in jurisprudence. "Nominalists" can achieve valuable things in a number of other areas; but they do not belong in the field of jurisprudence.

II

If jurisprudence is to warrant once more the appellation of a *science*—that is, as the international result of international collaboration, independent of political parties and economic special interests—then it must elevate itself above the mere technique of working over the statutes of positive law belonging to this or that state, and, instead, elaborate a *universal theory of law*, which would form part of the positive legal systems of individual states, rather as the "universal part" of the *Bürgerliches Gesetzbuch* relates to the other parts of that code.

The completion of this task (a task which, in reality, is faced by every science)[2] will only be possible, however, when jurisprudence stops wanting to be a kind of natural science, when it stops taking the mere *facts* of positive law as a kind of "natural given," and basing its work on these facts instead of basing itself on the ideals, ideas, and concepts of *law itself*, and creating *norms* that will stand to the statutes of positive law as, for example, algebraic procedures with general quantities stand to the arithmetical calculation of particular sums.

As a science of pure norms, the object of jurisprudence is not "being" but what "ought to be." This Ought, however, only ever appears as an "ought" in relation to empirical reality; it is acquired from the realm of being of ideal values, which is superordinate to the being of empirical reality. For this reason, jurisprudence, if it is to be true to its vocation, posits methodological requirements of a particular kind. Like theology, jurisprudence demands the ability to grasp certain metaphysical realities in such a way as to produce unshakable conviction. The jurisprudentialist must become *rechtsgläubig*, that is, a devout believer in law, through *episteme*, the immediate intu-

---

[2] Natural science, mathematics, history, philosophy, and theology have a universal validity; there is, for example, neither a national mathematics, nor a national theology.

ition of legal values. Like philosophy, jurisprudence demands the capacity for disciplined and principled thinking by means of universal concepts, Plato's *dianoia*. Like natural science, jurisprudence, in its applied aspect, obliges its practitioners to have a feeling for facts and for diagnostic and prognostic reasoning, a procedure based upon comprehensive knowledge of political, social, and economic relationships, and of human life in general—the capacity for Plato's *doxa*.

The whole field of jurisprudential work, accordingly, consists of *three* "layers" or "levels":

(1) *The knowledge of law*—here *law itself* is known, and becomes a creative impulse igniting the will.

(2) *The discipline of law*—here all the consequences of the knowledge of law are drawn and are organized into an intellectual system.

(3) *Legal policy*—here legal norms are fitted to current relationships by legislation, and by the interpretation and application of law, to the end of the realization of a just social order.

The restoration of the *three-level structure* of law is therefore a precondition—one which is in practice lacking today—for the regeneration of jurisprudence. The philosophy of law is today separated off as a distinct field and shuffled off into the domain of philosophy, which means that only the level we have called "legal policy" remains, as "actual" jurisprudence. Once separated from the theology of law and the philosophy of law, however, legal policy is like a body without a spirit or a soul. It then lacks the warmth of moral feeling, and the orienting light of the highest values of human culture.

The philosophy of law, therefore, must not be permitted to be split off as a special area given over to those who are interested in it. Its significance must be that of the (in reality self-evident) obligation to give oneself an account of the essence of that which one is intending to work on, to practice, and to represent, and to give an account, too, of its relationship to the other values of human culture. The philosophy of law should therefore not only be thought of as the "universal part," as it were, of all the other areas of jurisprudence, but should—precisely as a "universal part"—*inform* all the specialist areas of jurisprudence. It must once again attain the significance of being the *foundation* upon which the whole building of jurisprudence is erected.

> Either there will no longer be any such thing as law, or law will appear in the light of reason as an organic element of the social world, an element that participates in the idea of the absolute, bearing, like the absolute, an eternal and invariable universal character imperiously and directly commanding that individual and collective personhood be respected and protected. Such is the choice before which a rational examination of the problem of law, in our view, places us: Law as a primary idea, as a manifestation of the absolute, or Law as non-existent.[3]

[3] Julien Bonnecasse, *La Nation de Droit en France au dix-neuvième siècle* (Paris, 1919), 219 [translated here from the original French].

Outline of the
Principles of a Reform
of Academic Training in Law

REGENERATION OF JURISPRUDENCE along the lines suggested in the preceding remarks will only be possible if academic *training* in law also undergoes corresponding changes. For the existing jurisprudential literature and the content of the lectures on, for example, the philosophy of law, will never be adequate to the task if the study of jurisprudence in universities is carried on according to the current plan. Only a drastic reform of the course of study itself, towards a method of studying individual topics that corresponds to the nature and tasks of jurisprudence, can crown efforts to regenerate jurisprudence with success.

If we look at a recent study plan for the law faculty, the striking fact is that "Philosophy of Law and the State (or System of Law)" is set to run only in the first semester, with two to four hours of teaching per week, and without any practical exercises, whereas, for example, economic science runs for five semesters, with, in total, eleven to fifteen hours of lectures and one to two hours of practical exercises per week. This fact shows very clearly what those who set up this plan of work imagined to be essential: the future lawyer is to be able to apply his legal training to the field of *economics* in particular. It is also a distinguishing feature of the plan of work that among the individual topics, which are listed in the plan as history, the nation, the corporate state, the business of law, legal protection, foreign law, philosophy of law, and economic science, only economic science runs for five semesters, while the other areas are awarded at most four semesters, and one, namely the philosophy of law, has only a single semester devoted to it.

If, however, setting aside political, national, and other special interests, we ask ourselves the purely pedagogical question of *what* it is essential for the student of jurisprudence to learn, we must first of all point to the fact that he first has to learn *to think for himself.* Secondary schooling, from which the student usually comes straight to university, does not suffice to equip him for the claims which the study of the law will make upon his capacity to think. For legal concepts are subtle and sharply defined; they demand a capacity to think which is capable of working comfortably with general concepts, and of discerning principles. School practice in mathematics, and school essays on literary-historical topics, are not a sufficient preparation for this.

When he embarks upon the study of jurisprudence, the student encounters a new world of concepts, for which his schooling has barely prepared him. It is different with the fields of, for example, the natural sciences, of history, of philology. There the student brings something along with him, from which he can make a start. For he has already to a certain degree absorbed physics, chemistry, botany and zoology, history, and the study of grammar, and is in a position to connect new material with what he already knows. But the student who commences the study of jurisprudence is in a different position. He can hardly find anything with which he can connect,[1]

---

[1] With one exception, however. If the student has had the advantage of instruction in the Roman Catholic religion, he will, in the *way* in which concepts are customarily treated in catechetical teaching, have something to hold on to: much of the spirit of jurisprudence is retained in the catechism.

and has to learn to swim in an element foreign to him. As an emergency measure, he seeks refuge in cramming.

For this reason, the *first task* is to make possible a transition from thinking based on universal principles to juristic thinking. The first part of this "bridge" from thinking based on universal principles to juristic thinking first has to be constructed and tested before one can pass on to its application to the field of jurisprudence. One must also become familiar with the world of *values* as such, the world to which these particular values belong, and to whose service the intending jurist is to devote the remainder of his life.

Jurisprudence, therefore, requires as a preliminary that the student think through, at the very least, those central problems of philosophy that are especially important for an understanding of the foundations of jurisprudence—for example, the problem of freedom, the ontological problem, the problem of values, the theological problem, and the ethical problem. It goes without saying that it cannot be a question either of knowing the entire massive field of the history of philosophy, or of the comparably vast task of studying all contemporary philosophical systems, but only of thinking through some of the most important philosophical problems, to the end of exercising one's independent thought, and, at the same time, of rendering more secure one's grasp of concepts that will later come up, both implicitly and explicitly, in jurisprudence.

The values in which law is rooted are, however, native to the realm of *religion*; and it is theology that possesses the method by which judgements of value are to be made, and by which values are to be ranked in a system of values according to their moral weight. It would therefore be necessary for preliminary study to be undertaken in the philosophy of religion, that is, in theology, simultaneously with work in philosophy, since only by means of this sort of simultaneous work can either the knowledge and right appreciation of spiritual values be attained (something that is indeed a *sine qua non* for a jurist), or, equally, the capacity to think independently in the service of these values be acquired, that is, the capacity to concern oneself in a fruitful way with the main problems of civilized life.

After this preliminary philosophical and theological work, whose task is to arrive at the capacity for principled, logical thinking, and for esteeming values according to their moral weight—that is, to be a preliminary to the later capacity for *moral* thought (which, in any case, only usually develops when one is of more mature years)—the study of jurisprudence proper can follow. It should first of all take the form of the philosophy of law, as a kind of "universal part," not only in relation to all the other individual specialized areas of jurisprudence, but also in relation to all the individual national legal systems of European and American civilization.

This *second stage* should be the real transition, from thinking in general concepts and values, to the application of this thinking to the field of law. The task here is to master the basic concepts of jurisprudence, such as, for example, law, the subject of law, the object of law, the legal relationship, etc., with enough thoroughness to be in a position, with the help of these concepts, to orient oneself in relation to the essential principles of any positive legal system (the principles of the law of the regions that adopted Roman law, for example, or of Swiss or English law, say) and to concisely formulate these principles from out of the mass of statutes.

It is precisely the point, here, to develop and exercise an ability to distinguish the essential from the inessential. The task of this level is not, however, limited to the development of this capacity; it is only half of the task to *acquire* principles from the material in front of one. The other half consists in bringing the principles thus yielded into concord with each other, to learn to systematize and to codify. This, however, will be best learnt by working with some particular example and model. This is to be provided by a *universal theory of law*, which would bring together all the principles of law as such. This universal theory of law would also contain the foundations of national law in natural law, so far as the latter underlies the positive legal systems of individual peoples—that is, it would bring together the *norms of the law of humanity*, in however incomplete a form.

The task of assisting students to develop certain *abilities*, rather than merely communicating information to them, brings with it a need to make much more intensive use of seminars and practical exercises than is currently usual. This holds especially for philosophical and theological preparation and for the philosophy of law, where it is a case of developing the use of those capacities which are to be the foundation for all further study—indeed for the whole later legal career of the student.

Since the essential task of the second stage consists in working through and learning to handle juridical concepts, an important aid to this is the part played by the *process* of learning these concepts that takes place within the students' consciousness. In order to learn to think juridically, Roman law, medieval canon law, and the common law of the nineteenth century are of inestimable value. A great injury has been done to the study of law in Germany by the suppression of the study of Roman law. This has deprived students of material to practice on, material which not only offers an excellent schooling in thinking in sharply defined concepts, but also has the value of forming one's language and style. Anyone who is unfamiliar with Roman legal sources in the original will hardly have another opportunity to come to know and to prize the verbally concise purity and clarity of this classic legal style.

The history of law, and of Roman law in particular, requires, if possible, that one know enough Latin to be able to read the sources in the original. There is no getting round this requirement: the student is best served by having immediate access to a two-thousand-year-old literature, which contains within itself the development of all civilized values. By acquiring a sufficient facility in Latin, one is rescued from the "temporal provincialism" of our age, a provincialism that consists in being familiar with, and taking seriously, only the last two centuries at most, while that which is contained in thousands of years of the past is squashed together into a quick overview.

It is not only "temporal provincialism" that needs to be overcome in our universities, however, but also, and especially, the "spatial" kind. It is certainly true that the German branch of jurisprudence has achieved an enormous amount, and that it rightly possesses an honorable place in jurisprudence. But it should never be forgotten that German jurisprudence is only a *branch* of jurisprudence, and that others in other countries, as well as here at home,[2] have also occupied themselves with German problems.[3] To this end it should be a requirement that each student should master at least one foreign language in both written and oral form—to a level well beyond what is possible today at secondary school, that is. So long as this is not made obligatory, the study of the law will be damagingly limited to national concerns, and jurists will be unable to stand as representatives of the whole of European Christian civilization, or as conscious participants in its tasks and trials of strength.

Only at the *third stage* of study would students be in a position really to work through the large body of material for study, to absorb it, and to assimilate it with an alert intelligence. And here too, indeed, the essentially juridical method of proceeding from the universal to the particular must be followed.

---

[2] Let us recall again that the Russian author is writing this text in war-torn Germany in 1944, under the direction of the German professor of Jurisprudence (who was as well the author's good friend) Ernst von Hippel. Ed.

[3] It is, for example, to be lamented that the work and debates of the *four* French schools of the study of law—the sociological, the psychological, the metaphysical, and the Catholic—are so little known in Germany.

Study should begin with national and ecclesiastical law, as the two areas of *human* law, in order then to get to know the comparative law of individual nations through its principles. Then the right time would have arrived, well equipped with the legal norms of the past and of other countries in the present, to work critically through positive national law. At this level it is not necessary to follow a particular sequence of individual areas of law; the student has been sufficiently prepared and enabled to get to know the different specialized areas of private and public law at the same time, since he will now be able to organize this extensive and manifold material by content; that is, not merely to retain it in his memory, but also to divide it up and to work through it logically.

The *fourth stage,* which is the last, has a double task. First, it is to prepare for the application of jurisprudence to the fields of political and economic life; second, it is to produce clarity about what is to be striven for in such an application, that is, about the goals and methods of *legal policy* as a means for the realization of a better state of society. Economics and social science, as well as political science and the study of governance (treated from the standpoint of the legal policy goals resulting from the whole course of study) would be added at this stage to the topics studied earlier.

If one takes an overview of the whole course of legal training from the perspective of the present outline of its fundamental reform, and of the demands made on students, it will clearly be necessary to considerably extend the time allotted to the study of jurisprudence.

* * *

If we now bring together the fundamental ideas underlying a reform of the study of jurisprudence, as developed in the foregoing discussion, we arrive at the following principles:

1. "Nominalism," as the incapacity to experience spiritual values as values, and as the refusal of moral and principled thinking, has no place in the field of jurisprudence. It must be banished from the schools of jurisprudence, as injurious to the latter's very nature and as endangering its future survival.

2. "Realism," as the capacity for and method of moral and principled thinking, corresponds, by contrast, to the essence of jurisprudence, and makes possible the continuation and further development of its traditional method of proceeding from the universal to the particular.

3. If jurisprudence is, as a science of norms, "realist," then the study of it must be constructed according to the nature of jurisprudence, that is, it must proceed from the universal and the principle to the particular and the concrete.

4. For this reason a general philosophical and theological preparation must precede the study of the philosophy of law and the study of private and public law. The study of the sphere of influence of legal policy must follow the latter, so that positions taken in legal policy follow from the whole course of study.

5. The main pedagogical aim of the course of study is to develop the abilities to think independently, both according to moral principles and jurisprudentially, that is, both analytically and synthetically.

6. The final goal of the course of study is the formation of jurists as people who can connect the highest ideal with the greatest wealth of specific facts, and who will embody the idea and the ideal of law, free from the

influence of what is merely national, of classes, and of economic and political interests.

7. In this way it can be hoped that the perilous influence of pure positivism, which degrades law into a means for the celebration of pure power and brings about the *degeneration* of jurisprudence, can be overcome; and that jurisprudence will once again ascend to the summits of reason, to natural law, which is the "image and likeness" of divine law.

Afterword

The Degeneration and Regeneration of Jurisprudence, by my late pupil and friend Valentin Tomberg, first appeared in 1946, that is, immediately after the Second World War, from the now defunct publishing house of Götz Schwippert in Bonn. It has long been completely unavailable.

Its appearance now in a new edition is therefore both justified and timely, since the hopes that were entertained after the end of the war for a moral renewal of common life have remained unfulfilled. In particular, the degeneration of jurisprudence, that is, the way in which its materialism has advanced to the point of computer-thinking, is, today, all too clear, and threatens the moral foundations of public order as well as those of the lives of individual citizens. In particular, the fact that thinking now takes place almost wholly along the horizontal axis of the world of the senses, without regard to the vertical axis of the religious and moral realm, and of natural law, has brought about the loss of almost all real bonds both in the state and in family life.

In this context, the work of Valentin Tomberg reprinted here possesses both contemporary relevance and fundamental significance; indeed, it may prove, in an age of general disorder and confusion, to have a purifying and renovating effect, at least in the realm of jurisprudence.

ERNST VON HIPPEL
Perscheid, Michaelmas 1973

www.ingramcontent.com/pod-product-compliance
Lightning Source LLC
Chambersburg PA
CBHW022027090426
42739CB00006BA/325